R00007 68284

D1109670

PN8421K5
                    00428188.
KNOPP, JOSEPHINE ZADOVSKY
TRIAL OF JUDAISM IN CONTEMPORARY

The Trial of Judaism in Contemporary Jewish Writing

The Trial
of Judaism in Contemporary
Jewish Writing

Josephine Zadovsky Knopp

University of Illinois Press
URBANA CHICAGO LONDON

Publication of this work was supported in part by a grant from the Andrew W. Mellon Foundation

© 1975 by the Board of Trustees of the University of Illinois
Manufactured in the United States of America

LIBRARY OF CONGRESS CATALOGING IN PUBLICATION DATA

Knopp, Josephine Zadovsky, 1941–
  The trial of Judaism in contemporary Jewish writing.

  Includes bibliographical references.
  1. Jewish fiction—History and criticism.   2. Judaism
in literature.   I. Title.
PN842.K5   809.3'3   74-18319
ISBN 0-252-00386-1

_428188

For My Parents

Acknowledgments

This work evolved from a doctoral dissertation at the University of Wisconsin, Madison, written under the direction of Professor Cyrena N. Pondrom. I owe a large debt of gratitude to Professor Pondrom for her patient guidance and especially for that unyielding insistence upon clarity without which no thesis might have emerged. I am thankful as well to the Comparative Literature Department of the University of Wisconsin for generously awarding me a dissertation fellowship that supported my work for the crucial year during which the principal ideas of the dissertation (hence of this book) began to crystallize.

In the later stages of the work Professor Byron L. Sherwin of the Spertus College of Judaica provided help both in conversation and through a number of manuscripts which he made available to me before their publication. His advice led to the introduction of new ideas which, in my view, have strengthened the book. Bette Howland's intelligent and careful reading of the manuscript for the University of Illinois Press led to significant improvements; her interest in my work led directly to its publication. I extend my thanks also to Frank O. Williams of the University of Illinois Press for his interest and suggestions, and to Mrs. Bonnie Depp for her meticulous reading of the manuscript.

Finally, I am grateful to my husband, Marvin, who acted as a sounding board for ideas throughout the writing.

Contents

Introduction 1

ONE   The Code of *Mentshlekhkayt*
and the Trial of Judaism 6

TWO   The *Shtetl:* I. B. Singer 30

THREE   The Holocaust: Nelly Sachs
and André Schwarz-Bart 56

FOUR   The Holocaust: Elie Wiesel 70

FIVE   Jewish America: Bernard Malamud 103

SIX   Jewish America: Saul Bellow 126

Afterword 157

Index 161

Introduction

It is by no means clear what sense is to be made of the Jewishness of a writer who neither uses a uniquely Jewish language, nor describes a distinctively Jewish milieu, nor draws upon literary traditions that are recognizably Jewish. . . .

One cannot, however, simply discount the possibility that some essentially Jewish qualities may adhere to the writing of the most thoroughly acculturated Jews.[1]

A great deal of literary criticism in the last two decades has focused on the difficult problem of isolating, describing, and defining the "essentially Jewish qualities" of Jewish writing, Jewish writers, and the Jewish protagonist. One critic has approached this problem by noting that an outstanding common feature of much significant Jewish fiction of the present day is its tendency to put "Judaism on trial." [2]

Discussing Michael Blankfort, Herman Wouk, Bernard Malamud, Philip Roth, and Jerome Weidman, Dan Vogel has made the interesting claim that "unlike any other com-

1. Robert Alter, *After the Tradition: Essays on Modern Jewish Writing* (New York, 1969), p. 18.
2. Dan Vogel, "The Modern Novel—Mirror of the American-Jewish Mind," *Tradition*, V (Spring, 1963), 225–241.

pendium of characters and happenings, the American Jewish novel cannot escape putting the authority of Judaism on trial." [3] A related observation has been made by Charles Glicksberg: "The truth is, contemporary Jewish-American literature rebels against orthodoxy while actively seeking some substitute faith." [4] While Vogel and Glicksberg have restricted their discussions to Jewish-American novelists, in a rather different context Franz Kafka made a similar remark in connection with Heinrich Heine: "An unhappy man. The Germans reproached him and still reproach him for being a Jew, and nevertheless he is a German, what is more a little German, *who is in conflict with Jewry. That is what is so typically Jewish about him.*" [5] There is here an indication that this notion of "Judaism on trial," more broadly interpreted, could have wider applicability, to modern Jewish novelists of various nationalities writing in several languages. Indeed, in modern Jewish fiction the trial of Judaism amounts to a central theme, linking, for example, Saul Bellow and Bernard Malamud, both of these with Philip Roth, and all three in turn with Isaac Bashevis Singer and Elie Wiesel. The presence of this theme serves to unify Jewish writing as seemingly disparate as the European novels of the holocaust and Jewish-American fiction (and therefore argues for the validity of the "Jewish novel" as a coherent literary genre).

The examination of the trial of Judaism as a force in modern Jewish fiction is the guiding principle of this study. The isolation and description of this theme in novel-writing are among its ultimate goals, as well as the insight such de-

3. *Ibid.*, p. 226.
4. Charles I. Glicksberg, "A Jewish American Literature?" *Southwest Review*, LIII (Spring, 1968), 202.
5. Gustav Janouch, *Conversations with Kafka* (London, 1953), p. 58; italics mine.

scription may afford into the range of major attitudes toward Judaism to be found expressed in the work of current Jewish writers. More specifically, I shall examine aspects of the work of Isaac Bashevis Singer, Elie Wiesel, Nelly Sachs, André Schwarz-Bart, Philip Roth, Bernard Malamud, and Saul Bellow from the point of view of the trial of Judaism, concentrating, of course, on those works which reveal its influence most strongly. These writers may be divided naturally into three groups: Malamud, Roth, and Bellow, representing the Jewish-American novel; Singer, with his fiction centered in the pre-Nazi Eastern European *shtetl*; and Wiesel, Sachs, and Schwarz-Bart, who write of the holocaust and its aftermath. Although the three types of fiction have their roots in a common past tradition and are bound together by historical continuity, each of the three has its unique concerns. Furthermore, each of the writers has his own point of view from which he looks at and evaluates Judaism, his own distinctive insights, colored by the circumstances of his life, into Judaism's religious and cultural traditions. Thus this choice of writers guarantees diversity in the discussion of the Jewish novel and provides evidence that the novel in which Judaism is put on trial is a reasonably widespread literary phenomenon.

The novels chosen for particularly detailed discussion and analysis are *The Magician of Lublin, The Gates of the Forest, The Fixer,* and *Mr. Sammler's Planet.* Aside from the need to achieve diversity and the fact that each of the works represents fairly the creative output of a writer of some importance, the novels were chosen because each one is about Jews in a clearly identifiable Jewish situation and/or milieu. It could be argued that this last criterion for selection reflects an unduly narrow viewpoint concerning the nature of the Jewish novelist. (Kafka's works, for example, do not satisfy it, yet much recent criticism views him as a "Jewish writer" with a peculiarly Jewish view of the world rather than as a writer who merely happens to be Jewish.[6]) However, this viewpoint is necessitated by the purposes of the present study, for it is difficult to imagine that a writer could, more or less explicitly, put Judaism on trial or express an identifiable point of view toward Judaism in his work without fitting this narrow description. (This is not to say that Kafka, for example, and others could not be viewed as "Jewish writers" on the basis of broad ethical considerations which reach beyond particular cultural ones.) Moreover, the application of this restrictive criterion carries with it an important positive advantage: namely, it circumvents abstraction and points directly to specific literary considerations, of situations and characters within the novels themselves.

This analysis will seek to shed new light on the question of what is uniquely Jewish about much current Jewish fiction and these novels in particular, to bring into relief the common dependence of these works upon an essential core of Jewish history, experience, tradition, and outlook, and, in so doing, to establish that the "Jewish novel" can be considered a meaningful literary genre.[7] At the same time the already quite visible "Jewish protagonist" should come into sharper focus as the agent through whom the trial of Judaism is engendered; he is the plaintiff, so to speak, in the trial. A further goal of the analysis is the exposure and delineation of the Jewish ethical code that J. C. Landis calls

6. Alter, p. 18. See also Evelyn Torton Beck, *Kafka and the Yiddish Theater* (Madison, Wis., 1971).

7. That we have been able to discuss Nelly Sachs's verse drama, *Eli*, within the same framework used for the novels indicates that the point of view we have adopted may be applicable to "Jewish literature" in general.

the code of *mentshlekhkayt*, rooted in ancient Jewish Law and identified strongly with the *shtetl* culture of Eastern Europe, as a powerful influence upon the Jewish novelist and especially as a decisive factor both in his bringing Judaism to trial and in achieving a resolution of the trial.[8]

8. J. C. Landis, "Reflections on American Jewish Writers," *Jewish Book Annual,* XXV (1967–68), 140–147.

ONE

The Code of Mentshlekhkayt
and the Trial of Judaism

Mentshlekhkayt has as its fundamental premise the innocence of man, man free of the sins of the Fall. It recognizes that within man run opposing tendencies toward good and evil, and that within this context man is completely free to choose. It rests its ultimate faith in man's basic goodness and the implicit assumption that, in the final analysis, he will always choose what is morally and ethically right. It believes in action as the path toward moral redemption and rejects notions of salvation based on faith in a savior. It is an ethic concerned with improving man's lot in this world and not with the salvation of his immortal soul. *Mentshlekhkayt* reflects the traditional Jewish view of Messianic redemption as "a hope for an earthly paradise of love and learning, [and] a Utopian vision of a region of social justice and decency. . . ."[1] To those who accept, perhaps even unconsciously, the ethical code of *mentshlekhkayt*, the concept of an "absurd" universe is foreign; to them the universe has a definite structure and meaning, evolving from (though not necessarily the same as) the structure and meaning to be found in the Talmud and

1. J. C. Landis, "Reflections on American Jewish Writers," *Jewish Book Annual*, XXV (1967–68), 144. Also relevant is Landis, *The Dybbuk and Other Great Yiddish Plays* (New York, 1966).

Torah of traditional Judaism. At least a part of this meaning resides in the code's implicit faith in the moral significance of man's actions, the faith that man has the power within him to effect changes in the world for good or for ill, and that he has the obligation to apply this power in the cause of good.

Mentshlekhkayt also encompasses the very strong sense of community that has traditionally been a feature of Jewish life. The paramount characteristic of this community feeling is the moral imperative of man's responsibility to his fellow man. In the Talmudic "Ethics of the Fathers" the universe is described as supported on three pillars: Torah, service to God, and responsibility to man. A careful reading of the "Ethics of the Fathers" reveals that Torah study is really intended to be the study of morality, and that service to God, in its fullest sense, includes of necessity "good deeds to men." Thus man's obligation to man emerges as the principal moral foundation of the universe. From the point of view of the ethic of *mentshlekhkayt* the transgression of Cain in denying his responsibility toward his brother, expressed in the famous rhetorical question "Am I my brother's keeper?," ranks in seriousness with the murder he has committed.

The code of *mentshlekhkayt* is an order, a Law in a world of chaos and suffering, and thereby brings sanity and significance to life. Landis emphasizes this and at the same time suggests the function of *mentshlekhkayt* in the process of bringing God to trial: "The morality of *mentshlekhkayt* becomes a compensation for suffering or a mitigation of it. It required everyone to be a *mentsh*—even God; and it did not hesitate to rebuke Him when it thought He was remiss." [2] An excellent example of the principle enunciated

2. Landis, *Plays*, p. 5.

here by Landis occurs toward the end of Elie Wiesel's *The Gates of the Forest*, in a tale of four rabbis who are together in a Nazi concentration camp. One of the four summons the other three for the purpose of convoking a special court to put God on trial: " 'I intend to convict God of murder, for he is destroying his people and the Law he gave them from Mount Sinai. I have irrefutable proof in my hands. . . .' The trial proceeded in due legal form, with witnesses for both sides. . . . The unanimous verdict: 'guilty.' " [3]

Of course, bitter rebellion against Judaism and the God of Israel is not an invention of Wiesel, nor is it a modern conception. Indeed, such rebellion from within a Jewish context has its roots in the prophets and the ancient and venerable sacred writings, including the Pentateuch itself; here God is rebuked by several major figures, beginning with Abraham and including Job, Moses, and Jeremiah:

> Right wouldest Thou be, O Lord,
> Were I to contend with Thee,
> Yet will I reason with Thee:
> Wherefore doth the way of the wicked prosper?
> Wherefore are all they secure that deal very treacherously?
> Thou hast planted them, yea, they have taken root;
> They grow, yea, they bring forth fruit;
> Thou art near in their mouth,
> And far from their reins.
>
> (Jeremiah 12:1–2)

Hasidic literature, too, is replete with stories in which God is accused of wrongdoing and becomes the defendant in a suit.[4] A typical example is one in which a tailor relates to the Berditschever Rebbe his Yom Kippur argument with

3. Elie Wiesel, *The Gates of the Forest* (New York, 1966), p. 195.
4. Louis I. Newman, *The Hasidic Anthology* (New York, 1963); see, especially, pp. 56–59.

God: "You wish me to repent of my sins, but I have committed only minor offenses: . . . But Thou, O Lord, hast committed grievous sins: Thou hast taken away babies from their mothers, and mothers from their babies. Let us be quits: mayest Thou forgive me, and I will forgive Thee." [5]

In these writings "the Jew asserts his moral equality with his Father," a notion unique to Judaism and "totally incomprehensible without a clear perception of . . . [the] unique covenant" that the Jews have with God, a covenant described succinctly by Wiesel as follows: [6] "The Jewish people entered into a covenant with God. We are to protect His Torah, and He, in turn, assumes responsibility for Israel's presence in the world. Thus, when our spirituality—the Torah—was in danger, we used force in protecting it; but when our physical existence was threatened, we simply reminded God of His duties and promises deriving from the covenant." [7] In fact, "so long as man is a partner with God in sustaining the moral universe, accusations can be hurled from below as well as from above." [8]

The accusation "hurled from below" in *The Gates of the Forest*, made only after many patient reminders to God in Wiesel's fiction "of His duties and promises derived from the covenant," is representative of one facet of the trial of Judaism in recent fiction. Another aspect which the trial may assume is indicated in Melvin Bernstein's description of Saul Bellow's *Herzog*: "It is a testing of the Jewish definition of life and living, of purpose and death in the world —nothing less. It is a novel of ancient belief tested against

5. *Ibid.*, p. 57.
6. Harold Schulweis, "Man and God: The Moral Partnership," in *Jewish Heritage Reader* (New York, 1968), pp. 118, 121.
7. Elie Wiesel, "Jewish Values in the Post-Holocaust Future," *Judaism*, XVI (Summer, 1967), 281.
8. Schulweis, p. 120.

modernism in the person of Herzog." [9] Broadly put, the trial of Judaism typically occurs when the protagonist, a Jew imbued since childhood with Jewish Law and/or Jewish custom, has come to a crisis in his life. Whether he has previously grown alienated from his Jewish background or embraced it is now of no consequence; in this time of crisis he falls back upon his Jewish heritage in seeking a solution. In some instances, Job-like, he challenges the God of Israel directly to provide an answer. In this process he submits the ancient laws, values, and customs of Judaism to a rigorous test, seeking to determine whether they can provide a reasonable background for living in the modern world, whether they offer a viable basis for dealing with the problems he encounters as he moves in the larger society and contends with its values.

A variation of this general description appears in Malamud's *The Assistant* in the figure of Frank Alpine, who is not Jewish and thus has no Jewish background to which to turn in time of need. However, in the course of the novel Alpine undergoes a subtle conversion to Judaism and is therefore, in a sense, *acquiring* a Jewish background.[10] In this case Judaism is tested by Alpine to determine whether it can serve as a basis for his future life, as, for example, in his close questioning of Morris Bober concerning the Jews: " 'What I like to know is what is a Jew anyway?' " and " '. . . why is it that the Jews suffer so damn much, Morris? It seems . . . they like to suffer . . . they suffer more than

9. Melvin H. Bernstein, "Jewishness, Judaism and the American-Jewish Novelist," *Chicago Jewish Forum*, XXIII (Summer, 1965), 281.

10. The Jewish background is really provided by Bober, whom Alpine emulates and whose way of life, including especially adherence to the moral outlook embodied in Judaism, he ultimately accepts as his own.

they have to.' " [11] In trying to cope with Alpine's questions, Bober stresses the importance of the Torah, of following Jewish Law. Alpine protests that Bober does not really follow the Law, that he fails to go to the synagogue, that he works on Jewish holidays, that he violates the dietary laws. At this point Bober introduces an important idea: to follow Jewish Law " 'means to do what is right, to be honest, to be good. This means to other people.' " [12] This interpretation of Jewish Law is an elaboration of his comment of a few lines before: " 'My father used to say to be a Jew all you need is a good heart.' " The order of progression here is a frequent one in discussions of Judaism. It proceeds from observation of the letter of the Law to observation of its spirit, from stress on ritual observance to stress on being just and upright. In fact, Bober has here presented the essence of the code of *mentshlekhkayt*. Given Alpine's purpose in questioning Morris, his response is not surprising: " 'I think that other religions have those ideas too.' " [13]

That they do is not open to serious question, and indeed Alpine's observation assumes significance as a challenge to delineate the unique features of Jewish morality (that is, of *mentshlekhkayt*) as opposed to Christian morality, the morality of classical (pagan) humanism, or even that of the more recent secular humanism. Any proper response to Alpine's implicit question must entail the Jewish view of man's nature and, ultimately, the covenant with God. Indeed, the code of *mentshlekhkayt* (we might call it Jewish humanism) derives from the idea of "the interdependence and interaction of the world, man, and God" which is "just

11. Bernard Malamud, *The Assistant* (New York, 1957), pp. 98–99.
12. *Ibid.*, p. 99.
13. *Ibid.*

as fundamental a tenet [of Judaism] as is their separate reality." [14] This interdependence finds concrete expression through the covenant with God and thus in the relationship of the Jews to God's Law (Torah).

For the theologically serious Jew the spirituality of organized conventional prayer within the synagogue is seriously diminished without concomitant dedication to morality within the mundane world of men. Indeed, man's good deeds, his moral acts as he moves among his fellow men, are themselves a form of prayer; whether or not he acknowledges God explicitly, in assuming responsibilities imposed upon him by the covenant, he indirectly affirms his allegiance to God himself. This is well illustrated by the commentary on Exodus of the Talmudist Rabbi Eleazar of Modiim: "He who transacts his business honestly and is pleasing to his fellow men is accounted as having fulfilled *the entire Torah*." [15]

It is illustrated as well by the figure of Job. As Robert Gordis has pointed out, Job is not a Jew, and thus the problem of his suffering is not reducible to questions concerning the violation of Jewish ritual law: "Job is a man of integrity and piety who fears God and eschews evil. No more need be said." [16] In the Book of Job it is ultimately a specifically *ethical* motif that dominates, as "Job looks forward to his moral vindication, not to his physical restoration." [17] It is Job's "burning conviction that man's suffering in the world

14. Manfred Vogel, "The Jewish Image of Man and Its Relevance for Today," in Alfred Jospe, ed., *Tradition and Contemporary Experience* (New York, 1970), p. 117.

15. S. S. Cohon, *Judaism: A Way of Life* (New York, 1962), p. 102; italics mine.

16. Robert Gordis, *The Book of God and Man* (Chicago, 1965), p. 45.

17. *Ibid.*, p. 61.

is an affront to the goodness of God," and in this his moral stance is a peculiarly Jewish one, rooted in the covenant and pointing toward the trial of God.[18] In the modern day Singer, Malamud, and Wiesel, among others, have in fact gone beyond Job's accusation of God to assert that if God fails to uphold his part of the covenant, then it is man's responsibility to take God's duty upon himself.

Thus, though the moral code of *mentshlekhkayt* is based upon the covenant, it acquires an independent reality, separate from Jewish theology or questions of ritual observance, while at the same time remaining "Jewish" as contrasted with secular. The moral Jew may find God's nature beyond his grasp, yet still adhere to his commandments; in the Jewish view the moral man need not even acknowledge the existence of the covenant to act in accordance with it. This contrasts markedly both with secular humanism, in which God (and hence the covenant) plays no role, and with the responsibilities imposed by Christianity, for which, "though deeds are important, the indispensable condition of salvation is faith." [19]

The contrast with Greek thought is of another kind. Beyond the rather obvious question of Jewish (and, of course, Christian) monotheism, with its implied universal brotherhood of man, there is a sharp distinction between the classical and the Jewish views of man's essential nature. While it is Plato's view that man's true essence is his spirit (soul) and Aristotle's that man is essentially of the material universe (body), Judaism holds that body and soul are inseparable elements of the single being and that man's essence

18. *Ibid.*, p. 62.
19. Alfred Jospe, "The Jewish Image of the Jew: On the Meaning of Jewish Distinctiveness," in Jospe, ed., *Tradition and Contemporary Experience*, p. 131.

is determined by both.[20] A further important distinction may be drawn. The Jewish tradition of rebellion against authority can be contrasted with Socrates' acceptance of death, in spite of the fact that he was innocent by his own definition of justice. Socrates' acceptance and affirmation of the higher authority in spite of the state's evil are juxtaposed to "the Jewish prophet who challenges the social order precisely because it is evil." [21] Indeed, bolstered by the ethical and legal force of the covenant, the Jewish prophet may (and sometimes does) challenge God himself. Thus "to do what is right, to be honest, to be good" derives a unique connotation from the Jewish context.

Moreover, the code of *mentshlekhkayt* is influenced by the traditional Jewish notion of "chosenness," which is properly interpreted in the light of sacred texts and commentaries thereon as an ethical charge: the Jews are chosen to show God's way to the rest of mankind and, frequently, to suffer for the sake of this good cause. To Alpine's question, " 'What do you suffer for, Morris?' . . ." Bober answers, " 'I suffer for you,' . . ." an answer echoed in Wiesel's formulation "I suffer, therefore you are." [22] Interestingly, Roth's embittered Portnoy exhibits this same sense of responsibility to his fellow man: "But who was there to rescue me? My *shikses*. No, no, I rescue *them*." [23] It is fair to conclude that the code of *mentshlekhkayt* is a product of *Jewish* history and *Jewish* Law, essentially unaffected by the great changes brought about by the rise of Christianity, and that the experience of *mentshlekhkayt* is, in the sense intended here, a Jewish one. While it goes without saying

20. Vogel, p. 115.

21. Jospe, pp. 130, 131.

22. Elie Wiesel, *The Town beyond the Wall* (New York, 1968), p. 100.

23. Philip Roth, *Portnoy's Complaint* (London, 1969), p. 260.

that very many non-Jewish writers are concerned with social justice, with man's relationship to his fellow man, it is
only in Jewish writers (and only in certain of these) that
one finds a point of view explicitly shaped by this particular
ethical code.

Like Alpine, all our protagonists are ultimately seeking
answers to the questions posed by Bellow—"How should
a good man live; what ought he to do?"—and testing Judaism with respect to its power to yield meaningful responses
to them.[24] It is in this context that the code of *mentshlekhkayt* has made its influence deeply felt. In fact, the entire
code can justifiably be interpreted as an attempt to deal
with this question. One could argue that *mentshlekhkayt*
goes far toward providing a vindication for Judaism, not so
much because it provides concrete answers but rather because, through the code, Judaism has provided an intellectual and moral climate in which the question can be
meaningfully considered, indeed, in which the question cannot be avoided, in which its consideration has become an
imperative. Thus the code of *mentshlekhkayt* serves a dual
function in the trial of Judaism, acting as a powerful stim-
ulus toward the creation of the trial on the one hand and,
on the other, supplying a point of view from which one can
begin to approach answers to the basic question which is
the subject of that trial.

In dealing with the problem of how a good man should
live, Singer, Wiesel, and Malamud inevitably fall back
upon the values embodied in the moral code: the belief
that a man has the right to fulfillment, the affirmation of
gentleness and repudiation of violence, the assumption of
responsibility of man for his fellow man. Malcolm Bradbury has referred to the work of Bellow in the following

24. Saul Bellow, *Dangling Man* (New York, 1960), p. 39.

way: ". . . a writing distinctively soul-searching . . . concerned with nothing less than the condition of man . . . concerned too with a heritage whose emphasis on learning, deep feeling and a *heavy sense of responsibility to other men* has coloured American intellectual life." [25] The essence of these remarks applies equally well to Singer, Wiesel, Malamud, and (to a lesser extent) Roth. All of them, in their concern for other men, in their compassion and emphasis upon right and moral action, are responding to the principal tenets of *mentshlekhkayt* and thus to a uniquely Jewish view of the world.

In the case of Roth, Jewishness, Jewish institutions, and Judaism as practiced by middle-class American Jews are often treated as irrelevant or even crippling to the Jew in America in the face of the problems that he encounters in the world. As such they prove themselves burdens to be discarded, hindrances which provide no real direction, no relevant guidelines for daily living. It is primarily in this sense that the trial of Judaism (and rejection of Jewish-American life) occurs in Roth's work. However, here again the code of *mentshlekhkayt* makes its influence felt: "The things that other men do—and get away with! And with never a second thought! . . . The indifference! The total moral indifference!" [26] Roth tests and finds wanting *Judaism* (the *Jewish* community, and no other), and from within the framework of a Jewish background, from the point of view of a member of the Jewish community, of one who knows and understands it well, rather than from the point of view of an uninformed outsider. Thus it is not a distortion to characterize Roth's viewpoint as a Jewish one.

25. Malcolm Bradbury, "Saul Bellow and the Naturalist Tradition," *Review of English Literature*, IV (Oct., 1963), 80; italics mine.
26. Roth, p. 273.

The circumstances under which the trial of Judaism occurs are quite different in each of the three fictional subtypes, and thus the immediate (although not the long-range) reasons for the trial are different as well. Given the unique makeup of the ghetto culture, it seems natural, upon reflection, that the literature emerging from the *shtetl* should incorporate as an important component a challenge to Judaism. For in the *shtetl* (and among Orthodox Jews in America as well) Judaism was very much more than a religion; it was indeed a way of life. For the Orthodox Jew, Judaism has something to say about almost every aspect of his life, from the most trivial to the most important. There are rules, indeed laws (and often appropriate prayers), connected with bathing, hand-washing, food (its preparation and consumption), relations with the opposite sex, treatment of one's family, labor relations, and a host of other subjects. In short, the Orthodox Jew leads a life dominated by the tenets of Judaism; inevitably, in moments of crisis he turns to his religion and his rabbi for aid and comfort, and for a practical solution to his currently pressing problems. If no solution is forthcoming, or if the proposed solution proves to be a failure, he may begin to doubt and question Judaism and his faith in it. He begins to question whether his reliance upon Judaism as a way of life was justified; in extreme cases he calls upon God directly to explain himself and his ways. This outcome is reinforced by the Jewish tradition of questioning God's relationship to man, of expectation that God fulfill his part of the covenant, of "faith in God's responsiveness to the call of justice." [27]

Within the context of this tradition it is easy to predict the literary effect of the circumstances of the daily life of the *shtetl*'s inhabitants. Although poverty was not the major

27. Schulweis, p. 121.

problem, many were poor. All were victims of repressive policies on the part of the national government and prejudice on the part of private citizens. Their freedom to travel was restricted and they were limited in a choice of livelihood. When there was not actual physical violence perpetrated against them, there was always the possibility and implied threat of such violence. The Jewish tradition of close examination, of questioning, of searching for a better answer—of testing Judaism—was given free rein under these circumstances and is reflected in the *shtetl*'s literary legacy as well.

World War II and the infamous "final solution to the Jewish problem" signaled the end of the *shtetl* and literally the end for most of its inhabitants. Eastern European Jewry was destroyed, virtually overnight, and with it the culture of the *shtetl*, only remnants of which remain in the United States and other countries where there are relatively large numbers of Jewish inhabitants. Out of this experience grew the novel of the holocaust, which witnesses, documents, and responds to the death of the *shtetl*, just as the *shtetl* novel witnesses its tenuous but rich and varied life. If there was cause to put the authority of Judaism on trial in the confines of the *shtetl*, there is all the more cause with its destruction. Thus we are not surprised to discover that a challenge to Judaism and to the God of Israel is a recurrent motif in the novels of Wiesel. Where, he wants to know, was God when children were separated from their families and made orphans, when parents were made childless, when entire families were destroyed? The questions are all the more compelling because Wiesel himself is a survivor of the holocaust, and his work is largely autobiographical. The trial of Judaism, as it occurs here, emphasizes a direct challenge to God and assumes an added dimension of poignancy and desperation which issues as a deeply felt response to a monstrous situation. Nevertheless, it is in the same tradition as the challenge to Judaism that occurs in the *shtetl* novel, and it can be best understood from that point of view.

If we concede without argument that there is a valid basis for the writer dealing with *shtetl* life or one describing the holocaust to put Judaism on trial, we may nevertheless wonder why the Jewish-American writer feels compelled to follow suit. Indeed, his "arrival" not only in American literature but in all aspects of American life would seem to preclude such a trial. In spite of his success, the Jewish-American novelist does subject Judaism and his Jewish background to close scrutiny, often challenging basic beliefs and customs and sometimes making Judaism and Jews the object of his mockery. This can largely be attributed both to the ancient Jewish tradition of challenge and to a form of "identity crisis" that the Jew in America frequently experiences. The origin of this crisis may be explained by comparing the American Jew with his ancestor in the *shtetl* of Eastern Europe. A Jew living in a Russian *shtetl*, for example, was by no means a Russian. He did not think of himself as a Russian, nor did his non-Jewish neighbors, nor did the czarist government that withheld from him the benefits (such as they were) of full-fledged Russian citizenship. Thus he remained unambiguously a Jew, with undivided loyalties and with little doubt as to his place in his society and in the Russian society at large.

This description offers a striking contrast to the situation in which the American Jew finds himself today. Jews came to America with the profound hope that here at last was a place where they could not only find relief from persecution but also find a real home and succeed in the larger society. To a surprising extent this early hope has found subsequent justification. In spite of difficulties, the Jew discovered that he could become (indeed, only with effort could he avoid becoming) a "real American," with a new set of values and a new outlook on life. Government took no special stand against him and his neighbors were often willing to accept him as one of them, turning against him only if he insisted on maintaining a separate Jewish identity. Not surprisingly, acculturation and assimilation occurred rapidly, especially among the second-generation Americans. With this assimilation many of the old traditions and customs carried over to America from the *shtetl* began to disappear, and with them, regrettably, the Yiddish language. The second generation were becoming Jewish Americans rather than merely Jews living in America.

This seemed a natural development and caused no particular concern until the destruction of European Jewish life in World War II and the subsequent establishment of the state of Israel. These events, of obviously far-reaching significance, forcefully and abruptly brought the importance of his ancestry into the consciousness of the American Jew. Thus as early as 1943 Albert Halper wrote: "Alas, my friends, I *am* different. Hitler has made me different . . . : when I now sit down to write a story, or a novel, . . . I hear the cries of five million expiring Jews outside my window." [28]

The old "homeland" of Eastern Europe was gone and a new one in the Middle East took its place. It became clear that the preservation of the *shtetl* culture, to the extent that it was possible at all, was largely in the hands of

28. Albert Halper, "Under Forty: A Symposium on American Literature and the Younger Generation of American Jews," *Contemporary Jewish Record* (1943), p. 23.

American Jews. This realization forced the American Jew to re-evaluate his own identity and to explore the nature and extent of his Jewishness, with the result that he began to resist total assimilation into the Gentile world. On the other hand, the process of acculturation had, in most families at least, gone too far to allow an abrupt return to the old ways. American Jews for the most part did not want to return to Orthodox Judaism and the ghetto existence, even were this possible: "For all the return to religion in the past fifteen years, the American Jewish community remains a community of citizens of Western civilization seeking Jewish roots rather than a community of Jews seeking a rapport with Western civilization." [29]

Thus it became important for each Jew individually to attempt to isolate explicitly those aspects of Judaism to be preserved in his personal life, and the resultant soul-searching is fully documented in the Jewish-American novel. The process of acculturation into American society within the context of a *shtetl* background has produced a unique combination of American and Jewish values with which a "serious" Jewish-American writer must contend. Inevitably he is forced to test his Jewish inheritance against the values of the larger society in which he lives, thus putting Judaism and his Jewishness on trial.

Obviously the genocide of World War II and the statehood of Israel are issues so crucial and large that the writer who happens to be Jewish is almost certain to be deeply affected by them, as indeed many like Albert Halper have personally testified. In the case of a writer like Elie Wiesel, himself a victim of the Nazis, this is self-evident. More to the point is the remark of Bernard Malamud, an American

29. Malcolm L. Diamond, "Jewishness and the Younger Intellectuals," *Commentary*, XXXI (Apr., 1961), 319.

Jew not directly involved in the destruction of European Jewry: "The suffering of the Jews is a distinct thing for me. I for one believe that not enough has been made of the tragedy of the destruction of 6,000,000 Jews. . . . Somebody has to cry—even if it's just a writer, 20 years later." [30] It is not rash to conclude that the creative output of many writers of Jewish background is influenced by these events, that their awareness of the unprecedented upheaval experienced by the Jews in the very recent past will continue to affect their fictional subject matter and the view of the world that is reflected in their writing, as well as their personal reactions to the fact of their Jewishness. It has been pointed out that this is the case even in the work of Isaac Bashevis Singer, who writes of pre-Nazi Europe: "It is impossible for us to forget that the people Singer writes about *were* overwhelmed by catastrophe; . . . the paradoxical fact is that while he has re-created Eastern European Jewish life for its own sake (as he had to, if the task were to be done at all), he has done this also in order to be able to ask repeatedly, incessantly, obsessionally, why it should have suffered destruction." [31]

It is important to keep in mind that persecution, exclusion, and disaster are by no means new influences upon the lives and literature of the Jews, that in fact such influences have historically been part of the Jewish scene and have played a major role in shaping Jewish tradition. Yitshok Peretz, considered by many to be the father of modern Yiddish literature, well before the recent holocaust aptly expressed the effect of the shared Jewish historical

30. Joseph Wershba, "Not Horror but 'Sadness,'" *New York Post* (Sunday, Sept. 14, 1958), M2. Interview.

31. Dan Jacobson, "The Problem of Isaac Bashevis Singer," *Commentary*, XXXIX (Feb., 1965), 50.

experience upon the consciousness of the individual Jew: "Is there a people . . . a wander-folk without fixed borders . . . that lives, suffers and does not perish; that is weak, attacked by the greatest and the strongest and does not surrender—then must such a people see differently, feel differently, have a different view of life, a different conception of the future of the world, of life, and of man. . . ."[32] It would appear that the notion of a historical Jewish consciousness, shared by individual Jews, bears directly and intimately upon the question of whether there is in fact a uniquely definable genre which we may term "the Jewish novel," whether there are in fact "Jewish writers" and "Jewish writing" displaying recognizably distinctive characteristics. In order to justify such categorization completely, it would be necessary to give a definition of, say, "the Jewish novel," one precise enough to include all of the novels one would want to include under that rubric and to exclude all those one would want to exclude.[33] It is by no means universally accepted that the "Jewish novel" as a literary genre is a defensible notion or that the Jewish writer is somehow essentially different from his Gentile colleagues. Especially in America many critics oppose the notion of a Jewish novel. Max Schultz, for example, says, ". . . there is no Jewish school of novelists now. There are only Jewish-American writers practicing their craft."[34] W. B. Fleischmann, when speaking of the notion of the "Jewish novel" in America, says that "Moses Herzog, Ph.D., could be Giorgio Esposito, Ph.D., Joe Malone, Ph.D., or Hermann Schmidt, Ph.D. He is that first generation American intel-

32. As quoted in Landis, "Reflections," p. 141.
33. Our own previous discussion of Judaism on trial and *mentshlekhkayt* of course does not qualify as definition or even attempted definition. It lies in the more modest realm of description.
34. Max F. Schultz, *Radical Sophistication* (Athens, 1969), p. 3.

lectual whom I have personally encountered—in Irish, Italian, and lower middle class Anglo-Saxon Protestant guise —. . . ." [35]

Implicit in these statements is a challenge to any concept of "Jewish writing" and "Jewish writers" as literary phenomena and the related challenge to define these phenomena if they in fact exist. Undeniably the problem of definition is a most difficult one, its difficulties rooted ultimately in the problem of defining the/a "Jewish world view." Nevertheless, I feel that the weight of evidence is on the side of an axiomatic assumption that there are indeed "Jewish writers" and "Jewish writing," an assumption implicit, for example, in the statement of Robert Alter: "One cannot, however, simply discount the possibility that some essentially Jewish qualities may adhere to the writing of the most thoroughly acculturated Jews." [36] I believe, moreover, that a convincing case can be made for these concepts, short of a precise definition.

The concept of "Jewish qualities," not necessarily within a literary context, has been a subject of lively interest among Jews themselves, including recently Freud and Kafka. Theodor Reik states in the introduction to his book *Jewish Wit* that his own feelings about Judaism are analogous to those of Freud:

Freud stated that he did not understand Hebrew, that he was utterly alienated from the religion of his forefathers— as from any religion—and that he was unable to share the

35. Wolfgang Bernard Fleischmann, "The Contemporary 'Jewish Novel' in America," *Jahrbuch für Amerikastudien*, XII (1967), 162.

36. Robert Alter, *After the Tradition: Essays on Modern Jewish Writing* (New York, 1969), p. 18.

belief in national ideals. Yet he had never disavowed being Jewish and did not wish to be different. But what, he continued, would he answer, if someone asked him, "What is still Jewish in you after you abandoned all those things common to your people?" He would reply, "Still very much, perhaps the main part of my personality." He admitted that he would be unable to put this essential thing into clear words. . . .[37]

On the occasion of his seventieth birthday, in 1926, Freud "asserted that neither religious faith nor national pride had tied him to Judaism. He had always been an atheist. . . . Yet, he continued, there remained enough other things that 'made the attraction of Judaism and Jews irresistible, many dark emotional powers, the more powerful, the less they could be put into words, as well as the clear awareness of an inner identity, the secret of the same inner construction.' " [38]

Kafka, when considering the part Judaism had in his writing, declared: "What have I in common with Jews? I have hardly anything in common with myself and should stand very quietly in a corner, content that I can breathe." Nevertheless, the critical evaluations of Kafka's work over and over again emphasize the point of view (with which one may or may not take issue) that "his particular mode of fiction would never have occurred to a Christian imagination." [39] Acculturated as Kafka was, he still spoke of himself, when referring to his position as an employee of a state-sponsored insurance agency, as the single "display Jew" in a "dark nest of bureaucrats." [40] At another point,

37. Theodor Reik, *Jewish Wit* (New York, 1962), p. 11.
38. *Ibid.*, p. 19.
39. Alter, p. 10.
40. *Ibid.*, p. 29.

when the Czech writer Gustav Janouch asked Kafka if he remembered the old Jewish quarter of Prague, Kafka answered: "In us all it still lives—the dark corners, the secret alleys, shuttered windows . . . we walk through the broad streets of the newly built town. But our steps and our glances are uncertain. Inside we tremble just as before in the ancient streets of our misery. Our heart knows nothing of the slum clearance. . . . With our eyes open we walk through a dream: ourselves only a ghost of a vanished age." [41]

The statements of Freud and Kafka together form a striking pair. Freud believes in the existence of unique Jewish qualities while at the same time freely confessing his inability to describe or define these qualities; Kafka staunchly denies any common Jewish denominator, but upon another occasion he reveals a deep, not to say passionate, emotional attachment to Jewish life and values. The link is unmistakable—both accept the uniqueness of the Jew, but on the level of the emotions rather than on the level of the intellect, and both feel themselves to be somehow different from their non-Jewish contemporaries. Perhaps there is here the germ of an explanation why critics such as Lewisohn, Fieldler, and Alter have taken for granted the genre of the "Jewish novel," and why those who have felt the need to attempt a definition of "Jewish writing" have met with only limited success. The fact is that the uniqueness of the Jew is sensed but not completely understood, deeply felt but not easily rationalized. It is not surprising that these same difficulties have made themselves felt on the literary level and beset attempts to answer the large questions, "What is Jewish writing as op-

41. Gustav Janouch, *Conversations with Kafka* (London, 1953), p. 47.

posed to writing by Jews?" and "What is a Jewish writer as opposed to a writer who is Jewish?"

The difficulties inherent in attempting to define Jewish writing are well illustrated, I believe, by two examples of attempted definition. The first of these is that of Ludwig Lewisohn: "A Jewish book is a book by a Jew who knows that his ultimate self is Jewish and that his creativity and that deepest self are one. Jewish literature consists of those books, written in whatever age or tongue, whose authors know that they were *jüdische Menschen,* that they were *homines judaici,* and who, in the great old phrase of Sir Philip Sidney, looked into their hearts to write." [42] The second definition is that of Alexander Steinbach:

> Jewish themes . . . must be the outgrowth of, or identified with, the collective Jewish ego as it has developed and matured over the centuries. It . . . combines all the spiritual, cultural and intellectual potentialities imbedded in the Jewish personality. . . . If . . . its emphasis is upon a dynamic conception of the spiritual nature of man, it qualifies as . . . Jewish content and comes . . . within the purview of Jewish writing. . . . Jewish writing reflects an ethical and spiritual single-purposefulness that began in the long ago with Jewish monotheism and attained its full realization in the espousal of the doctrine of the brotherhood and unity of mankind. [43]

Both proposed definitions, while vague and abstract (and probably of little use to either the literary critic or the casual reader of fiction), hint strongly at the code of *mentshlekhkayt,* for those who look "into their hearts to

42. As quoted in Harold W. Ribalow, "The Jewish Side of American Life," *Ramparts,* II (Fall, 1963), 24.
43. Alexander Steinbach, "Themes for Jewish Writing," *Jewish Book Annual,* XVI (1958–59), 87.

write," or espouse "the doctrine of the brotherhood and unity of mankind," do in fact respond to the moral code. In fact, it has been suggested that the code of *mentshlekhkayt* is likely to play an important role in *any* definition of "Jewish writing": "To rehearse these ethical values is to spell out the moral platform of contemporary Jewish writing and to define its essential Jewishness." [44]

It can with justice be claimed that the failure to define the Jew's unique qualities on an intellectual level does not argue against the existence of "Jewish writing" or "Jewish writers." What I mean to suggest is that to the extent that a *feeling* of difference impinges upon the imaginative quality of the artist, to that extent will a genuine difference emerge in his creative work. Thus to the extent that writers of Jewish background, of whatever nationality, share a common feeling of racial and cultural uniqueness, to that extent does the "Jewish writer" come into existence, and to that extent are we justified in referring to "Jewish writing" or even the "Jewish novel."

The conclusions that emerge are that his Jewish background and experience do indeed make Moses Herzog (Ph.D.) essentially different from Giorgio Esposito, Joe Malone, and Hermann Schmidt (all Ph.D.s), that he is set apart from them as they are not set apart from each other by virtue of his history of expulsion, wandering, existence at the periphery of society, persecution, and the resultant questioning of God's ways to man; that the notions of "Jewish writer," "Jewish writing," "Jewish protagonist," and the "Jewish novel," as types, are indeed supportable on the internal literary evidence; and that although precise *definition* of the "Jewish novel" may be beyond reach,

44. Landis, "Reflections," p. 144.

description is well within it. In this connection the theme of "Judaism on trial" proves most useful. In isolating and describing this theme and its relationship to the code of *mentshlekhkayt* in modern Jewish fiction, one has in fact moved in the direction of characterizing the Jewish protagonist and describing the Jewish novel itself.

TWO

The *Shtetl*: I. B. Singer

The attitude toward the Jewish experience which emerges from the fictional works of Isaac Bashevis Singer, which indeed constitutes the philosophical underpinning of these works, may be characterized as one of ambivalent acceptance and admiration of the life and Jewish values of the Eastern European *shtetl*, a society which was destroyed in the holocaust but whose culture lives on, in small measure, among Jews in other parts of the world. Singer is not blind to the shortcomings of life in the *shtetl*, and as even the most superficial reading of Singer reveals, his acceptance is not an easy one, tempered as it is by his keen awareness of the tragedies of *shtetl* life, often the result of unreasoning superstitious belief. Singer is sensitive, however, to the great diversity available within the physically circumscribed confines of the *shtetl*, to the importance attached to the intellectual life, and to the highly developed sense of morality which is a response to the Jewish code of *mentshlekhkayt*, developed to its ultimate fruition in the receptive *shtetl* climate.[1]

But for Singer, too, the *shtetl* provides a natural setting within which Judaism may be put on trial, especially since

1. For a thorough treatment of the culture of the *shtetl*, see Mark Zborowski and Elizabeth Herzog, *Life Is with People* (New York, 1951).

the *shtetl* inhabitants respond to Judaism not merely as a body of religious belief and law but rather as a way of life. The incursion of Judaism into every minute aspect of *shtetl* life ultimately proves to be Judaism's vindication for Singer, as he describes with some sense of wonder the daily life of a people influenced at every turn by the rituals, customs, superstitions, and laws of the ancient religion of their ancestors. For the inhabitants of the *shtetl*, Judaism as a way of life provides a link with their past history, just as Singer's preoccupation with *shtetl* life in Eastern Europe establishes his own link with the past.

The autobiographical volume *In My Father's Court,* in which the author recalls his childhood in Warsaw, reveals how frequently Singer demanded that the validity of Jewish belief be substantiated in his own early trial of Judaism. "For [his] Father the answer to all questions was God," but Singer asks, ". . . how did he know there was a God, since no one saw Him? But if He did not exist, who had created the world, how could a thing give birth to itself? And what happened when someone died? Was there really heaven and hell?" And he adds, "I do not recall a time when these questions did not torment me." [2] Later Singer, then exposed to Polish anti-Semitism, seriously questioned the ways of God: "what did the Emperor of everything, the Creator of Heaven and Earth require? That He could go on watching soldiers fall on battlefields?" [3] It is not surprising that Singer's fictional characters are plagued by these same questions. "From childhood on" Jacob in *The Slave* "had been searching for the meaning of existence and trying to comprehend the ways of God. . . . An all-

2. Isaac Bashevis Singer, *In My Father's Court* (New York, 1967).
3. *Ibid.,* p. 173.

powerful Creator did not need to be sustained by the agony of small children and the sacrifice of His people to bands of assassins." [4] And of Asa Heshel in *The Family Moskat*, Singer writes that "the eternal questions never gave him rest." [5]

However, we may not easily infer from this questioning of Judaism a disbelief in God or diminution of faith on the part of either the author or his fictional characters. As Singer himself has pointed out, he has "always loved Judaism and . . . always believed in God." [6] What we may safely conclude is that, like the characters he portrays, Yasha Mazur and Jacob of Josefov, Singer is unwilling and unable to accept Judaism passively, as a body of fixed, unchallengeable law, custom, and dogma; rather, he must actively seek out the essential features of Judaism and the special Jewish relationship to God, testing the validity of Judaism as a guide to life. In the final analysis what survives the testing—for Jacob, for Yasha, and perhaps ultimately for Singer—is the Ten Commandments, the foundation upon which Judaism stands and the ultimate basis of the code of *mentshlekhkayt*.

Singer has referred to himself as standing outside the classical Yiddish literary tradition.[7] On the other hand, although Singer does not associate himself intimately with the traditional Jewish literary concerns, he nevertheless employs the culture of the Jewish *shtetl* as a backdrop against which he develops his own unique literary interests. At least this much, then, Singer shares with the classical

4. Isaac Bashevis Singer, *The Slave* (New York, 1967), p. 49.
5. Isaac Bashevis Singer, *The Family Moskat* (New York, 1967), p. 27.
6. Cyrena N. Pondrom, "Isaac Bashevis Singer: An Interview, Part II," *Contemporary Literature*, X (Summer, 1969), 350.
7. *Ibid.*, p. 349.

literary tradition of Mendele Mocher Seforim, Sholom Aleichem, and I. L. Peretz, which also has its center in the *shtetl*. The duality in Singer's relationship to the Yiddish literary tradition has been observed before. The literary *shtetl* of Singer has been referred to as "both reminiscent of and strangely different from that of the Yiddish classicists." [8] In contrast to the organized social community the classicists portray, the *shtetl* as Singer sees it "is not a community at all but a society in disarray." [9] In other words, the classical trio of Mendele, Aleichem, and Peretz, unlike each other in terms of theme, style, and literary attitude, are similar in that all three are social writers. That is to say, they are concerned with social conditions within the *shtetl*, both those which are determined by the alien, somewhat hostile outside world, and those conditions which arise from the *shtetl* context itself. Both Mendele and Peretz were strongly influenced by the Jewish Enlightenment known as the Haskalah, and both were dedicated to the idea "that the *shtetl* life of nineteenth-century East European Jewry needed to be changed drastically . . . and that reform and progress were not only essential, but also possible." [10]

8. Eli Katz, "Isaac Bashevis Singer and the Classical Yiddish Tradition," in Marcia Allentuck, ed., *The Achievement of Isaac Bashevis Singer* (Carbondale, Ill., 1969), p. 20.

9. *Ibid.*

10. *Ibid.*, p. 16. According to Katz, "All of the classicists in their different ways were concerned with the vast discrepancies between the community which ought to have been fostered by the precepts and practices which are virtually built into the traditional Jewish ethic—and what was the actual state of affairs" (17). For additional information on the social conditions at the time, see Mendele Mocher Seforim, *Fishke the Lame* (New York, 1960), and Charles A. Madison, *Yiddish Literature: Its Scope and Major Writers* (New York, 1968), p. 54.

The poverty of the *shtetl* during the period of the classical Yiddish writers was acute and living conditions wretched. While the squalor seemed to have little harmful effect upon the religious, cultural, and educational life of the *shtetl*, Mendele, for one, asserted that the toleration of these squalid conditions testified to the greed, ignorance, and complacency of the Jewish civic leaders. In our terms, what Mendele is concerned about here is the failure to live in accordance with the code of *mentshlekhkayt* on the part of a number of Jews of the *shtetl*, and his literary efforts directed toward the improvement of social conditions may justifiably be viewed as an attempt to guide these people back on the path of *mentshlekhkayt*. Among the classical Yiddish writers, *mentshlekhkayt* is discussed not only as an antidote to the social ills of the *shtetl* but, as well, as a positive virtue to be pursued for its own sake. Thus did Sholom Aleichem in his concern for the *shtetl* insist upon its communal tradition, defend its life style, and exhibit the Jews' "urge to dignity." Indeed, it has been claimed that Sholom Aleichem embodies the *"idealistic element* of Jewish history in the character of the *shtetl* folk." [11]

In contrast to the Yiddish classicists, Singer's literary *shtetl* and his point of view do not center on the evil that resides in social laws and conventions. He does not specifically call for social change, as Mendele and Peretz do. But, like them, he presents the *shtetl* "in all its peculiarly grotesque beauty and ugliness, spirituality and vulgarity," portraying only incidentally the evil effects of poverty and squalor on human beings.[12] Even more important is Sing-

11. Irving Howe and Eliezer Greenberg, eds., A *Treasury of Yiddish Stories* (New York, 1958), p. 54; italics mine.

12. Ben Siegel, "Sacred and Profane: Isaac Bashevis Singer's Embattled Spirits," *Critique*, VI (Spring, 1963), 30.

er's concern with the reality of the supernatural and the effects of evil manifestations, both natural and supernatural, on the human soul. He employs the supernatural as he does the rational; both are admitted as causal factors in the explanation of events.

While Mendele, Peretz, and Aleichem provide a clear and detailed picture of *shtetl* culture and society, Singer, on the other hand, is not primarily concerned with *shtetl* life on a rational, descriptive level. The center of Singer's *shtetl* actually lies in the irrational, in the demons, imps, and dybbuks, in the forces of good and evil that struggle for dominance over man's soul. Singer focuses upon his characters' psychological motivations and their reactions to affliction. The supernatural visions with which Singer's characters are beset often take on importance in the action, for they determine the manner in which these characters understand truth and reality. In this way Singer creates a literary situation in which "the supernatural is not simply another world, another reality, but primarily an extension of the problematic morality of this world." [13] Here Singer is opposed to his classical predecessors, who had no patience with the numerous superstitious beliefs and practices that were prevalent in the *shtetl*; Singer accepts *shtetl* life as a whole, the profane with the sacred, the superstition as well as the reverence for God's Law. His entire point of view is strongly colored by the explicit assumption that irrational, supernatural forces beyond reason or justice are active in the affairs of men, both within and without the *shtetl*. It is a corollary that Singer accepts evil as a natural component of man's God-given makeup, and it is the role of the code of *mentshlekhkayt* to contain and overrule this

13. Michael Fixler, "The Redeemers: Themes in the Fiction of Isaac Bashevis Singer," *Kenyon Review*, XXVI (1964), 372.

evil component. In this respect, again, Singer is markedly distinct from his predecessors, who tended to treat the evil existent in a character primarily as a natural response to an evil society.

The novel *Satan in Goray* provides a good example of the more subtle, dual nature of Singer's approach to the problem of evil. Goray, a *shtetl* in Poland, was besieged and its inhabitants almost completely annihilated in the Chmelnicki massacre of 1648. Eighteen years later, a recently rebuilt Goray is once more threatened by anti-Semitism. As it happens, it is also the year the cabalists have cited for the coming of the Messiah, and the people of Goray have seized upon the Sabbatai Zevi as the promised Messiah come to earth. They are deaf to the warnings of Rabbi Benish Ashkenazi, who stands virtually alone in his traditional piety, proclaiming that "so long as I live, there will be no idolatry in Goray" (27).[14] The people prefer to follow Reb Gedaliya and Reb Itche Mates, spokesmen for the Sabbatai Zevi, and under their leadership traditional values are discarded and learning is abandoned. When, later, the "Messiah" is exposed as a fraud, Goray is left in a state of complete disarray, its people burdened by an almost insurmountable sense of guilt.

J. A. Eisenberg has attempted to explain the actions of the people of Goray on the grounds that they were "weakened after years of murder and terror" and that the desire to believe their suffering was at last coming to an end was so strong that it rendered them easy victims to the lure of the "more relaxed and exciting spiritual rule" of their new leaders.[15] However, this is only a partial explanation,

14. Isaac Bashevis Singer, *Satan in Goray* (New York, 1963).
15. J. A. Eisenberg, "Isaac Bashevis Singer—Passionate Primitive or Pious Puritan?" *Judaism*, II (Fall, 1962), 348.

for Singer makes it quite clear that the wish to give way to
sensual passions, to commit adultery and lechery, was in
fact ingrained within the very souls of the Goray inhabitants, and that their hidden but real desire to let evil hold
sway allowed Satan to penetrate the walls of Goray. We
are told, for example, that the "new ruling [of Reb
Gedaliya] disagreed with the practices cited in the Shul-
chan Aruch, but the few learned men who remained pre-
tended neither to see nor hear what was happening . . ."
(112). It is, then, the combination of external evil forces
with the receptiveness to evil of the inhabitants that leads
to Goray's downfall.

Singer has explicitly expressed the belief that "man is
born bad, with a certain goodness in him, which he can
enhance and which he can completely destroy. . . ." [16]
Clearly this statement does not indicate passive acceptance
of man's inherited evil nature, nor does it deny the basic
assumptions of *mentshlekhkayt*; on the contrary, it constitutes a challenge to man to combat the evil aspect of his
nature and to nurture the good within himself. Singer's
fiction provides several important examples of characters
who take up the challenge and struggle against their own
darker instincts, among them Jacob, the central character
of *The Slave*, who thinks of himself as "small and sinful
and immersed in the vanities of the body" (55). A religious
Jew with a forbidden desire for the Christian girl Wanda,
Jacob prays to God for relief, even through death if necessary: "Lord, of the universe, remove me from this world,
before I stumble and arouse Thy wrath." "He had now
become a man at war with himself," Singer tells us. "One
half of him prayed to God to save him from temptation,
and the other sought some way to surrender to the flesh"

16. Pondrom, p. 336.

(35). Through Jacob, Singer imparts his feeling that man's basic struggle grows out of the tension between the evil which is part of his nature and his system of morality. It is evident that if man is successful in the struggle to have the good in him dominate the internal evil, then he is well prepared to withstand the evil imposed from without by society. Although Singer calls for the triumph of morality over evil, he gives no specific prescription for the accomplishment of this desirable end. Rather, he restricts himself to the assertion, which may serve as the moral foundation of all his writing, that "you are a good man if you don't make people suffer. This is the only measure; there is no other measure." [17] Indeed, what has been spelled out repeatedly in Singer's fiction is that "the approved way of life is that which causes least harm to others, a way wide enough to include Gimpel and Yasha as well as Asa Heshel and Itche Mattes." [18] Jacob, too, may serve as a literary model for this philosophical point of view: "If only I could live in perpetual summer and do harm to no one . . ." (105). And Yasha, the title figure of *The Magician of Lublin*, offers the advice for man's betterment: " 'Harm no one. Slander no one. Not even think evil' " (237). In asking that man not make his fellow man suffer, Singer is, in essence, pleading for life in accordance with the moral code of the *shtetl* society of which he writes. Indeed, Singer's fiction is largely preoccupied with the consequences of the loss of *mentshlekhkayt*, the struggle to regain it, the role of Judaism in this struggle, and the resulting trial of Judaism.

In order to understand this theme we need only look once more at *Satan in Goray*, in which all of these concerns are operative. This novel presents three separate aspects of

17. *Ibid.*
18. J. S. Wolkenfeld, "Isaac Bashevis Singer: The Faith of His Devils and Magicians," *Criticism*, V (Fall, 1963), 358.

Judaism, personified in the three figures of Rabbi Benish Ashkenazi, a rationalist who strictly observes the Jewish Law; Reb Itche Mates, a devoted cabalist; and Reb Gedaliya, who is essentially a Hasid. Singer shows, in the fall of these three men, that these particular brands of Judaism (and, by implication, all religious systems), when carried to fanatical extremes, can violate the code of *mentshlekhkayt* and render themselves invalid as guides to living.

The year 1666 is a bad one for the inhabitants of Goray, and as the cold season approaches, the poverty of the village makes itself even more acutely felt. Rabbi Benish, the leader of the community, is unable to effect any relief, and, in addition, there is once more fear that the Cossacks will attack the town. The news of the Sabbatai Zevi, the presumed Messiah, worsens matters, since in anticipation of his coming the inhabitants of Goray allow their physical surroundings to fall into complete disorder and the people themselves sink into eroticism and indolence. Rabbi Benish tries unsuccessfully to lead his people back to observation of the Jewish Law and to dissuade them from adopting the mystical teachings of the cabalists, who promise that the Messiah's coming is imminent. Frustrated, he becomes increasingly melancholy, until he finally secludes himself in the study house, away from both family and community, devoting all his energies to the study of the Talmud.

By Jewish Law and tradition, Rabbi Benish's self-imposed exile, even for the purpose of devoting all his time to the study of the Talmud, constitutes a transgression, a failure to meet his responsibility to his family, community, and fellow man. Thus "his descent into melancholy is accompanied by the historical sin of isolation from the family and from the community." [19] Consequently, Rabbi Benish's

19. Irving Buchen, *Isaac Bashevis Singer and the Eternal Past* (New York, 1963), p. 90.

strict construction and observance of the Talmudic Law is partially nullified from the religious point of view, for in his withdrawal from the community he has violated the very essence of the Talmud, the code of *mentshlekhkayt*.

A second example of the loss of *mentshlekhkayt* is afforded by Reb Itche Mates, a follower of the Sabbatai Zevi. Capable of fasting from one Sabbath to the next, sitting for many hours in contemplation of a single hair from his beard, he has completely immersed himself in the supernatural and has adopted an ascetic existence. So consumed is he by his passion for the mystical, in fact, that he is rendered impotent, both metaphorically and literally. His extreme piety becomes a source of pain and humiliation to his bride, Rechele, who is both disappointed and terrified by his behavior. The worst of it is that "when the seventh day of the Seven Days of the Marriage Feast was passed, Rechele was still a virgin," and she becomes the object of pity and mockery in Goray (95). Reb Itche Mates has humiliated his bride and violated the "principle of principles," "to be fruitful and to multiply" (93).

Reb Gedaliya, Singer's third example of the loss of *mentshlekhkayt* among the religious leaders of the *shtetl*, is the very opposite of an ascetic, for like the Hasids of a later period, he "hated sadness and his way of serving God was through joy" (104). But, like the other two, Reb Gedaliya carries his religious enthusiasm to the point of violating the code of *mentshlekhkayt*. Motivated by the fervor of his expectation of the Messiah's arrival, by the desire for power and lust for Rechele, he delivers a sermon "on the Great Sabbath before Passover" encouraging the people of Goray to adopt a new sexual freedom. His effect on Goray is overwhelming: "Twelve-year-old brides walked the streets with swollen bellies, for pious women saw to it that their daughters and sons-in-law lay with each other often" (119). For his part, Reb Gedaliya settles Rechele, the wife of Reb Itche Mates, in his house, and lies with her each night. Thus Gedaliya represents the perversion of the body in the same way that Mates represents the perversion of the soul, and Benish, in concentrating upon Talmud study to the exclusion of all else, even the welfare of the community, the perversion of the intellect.

In this novel Singer has put Judaism on trial by exposing the danger to religious and ethical values and to Judaism's followers of perverting faith through fanatical attachment to a particular sectarian point of view. Likewise there is the paradox that the anticipation of the coming of the Messiah sets in motion in the *shtetl* of Goray the forces of decay and disorder, when in fact it should have acted to draw the people together, as a homogenizing force.[20] This decadence is an indictment both of the people of Goray and of Judaism, and serves as evidence that Judaism can be a viable life guide only when its moral foundation, the code of *mentshlekhkayt*, is pursued. Without this foundation, Judaism may become a despotic, tyrannical force, as in Goray, where the Messiah assumes the aspect of Satan, and the three spiritual leaders become Satan's emissaries. In their surrender to the inner potential for evil, these three demonstrate that decadence resides as much within their own hearts as in the false Messiah.

The evil effect is compounded by their failure to recognize within themselves this evil potential, even after it has been converted into evil deed. They do not sense that their actions do violence to the foundations of Judaism, the religious and ethical system which they are committed to uphold, and indeed they continue to consider themselves

20. *Ibid.*, p. 93.

among the holiest of men. Jacob, in *The Slave*, observes the same phenomenon at work when he notes that "men like Gershon cheated, . . . slandered their fellow men, but demanded meat doubly kosher" (203). In *Satan in Goray*, as in *The Slave*, Judaism is tried through those who, consciously or not, hide the loss of *mentshlekhkayt* behind a mask of piety, those who substitute ritual for ethical purity.

Singer's *The Magician of Lublin*, a novel set in the nineteenth-century *shtetl* of Lublin, in Poland, may also be meaningfully viewed as a study in the trial of Judaism and the code of *mentshlekhkayt*. Yasha Mazur, the protagonist and a most unusual man by *shtetl* standards, is a magician, set apart from his fellows by both temperament and calling. He is capable of feats beyond the reach of ordinary men, beyond their imagining, in fact. For Yasha is no ordinary magician performing the usual pedestrian sleight-of-hand tricks that are the stock-in-trade of dozens of traveling "magicians." Indeed, "some maintained that he practiced black magic and owned a cap which made him invisible, capable of squeezing through cracks in the wall . . ." (5). His mind is described as a battleground upon which the powers of light and darkness are pitted against each other; he always "felt the wrangling of the forces within him, the good and the evil" (100).

Yasha serves as the agent through whom Judaism is put on trial in this novel, as within him there evolves a struggle between acceptance of Judaism and his traditionally Jewish *shtetl* background and their rejection, and a parallel clash between his inner capacity for evil and his personal sense of morality. The work can, in fact, be understood in terms of Yasha's reactions to these developing internal conflicts, his consequent attempts to understand the nature of divine power, and his ultimate resolution of the conflicts.

Structurally, the novel can be divided into three parts, the first of which presents a portrait of Yasha, describing his desire for complete freedom of action and the opposed influence of his *shtetl* background, his own standards of morality, which tend to act as restraints upon him. In the first part of the novel Yasha is presented as a Faustian figure with an almost insatiable need for knowledge and desire to impose his will upon nature. Yasha's powerful inner drives lead inevitably to the novel's second section, set in Warsaw, in which the previously internal conflicts force themselves to the surface. In Warsaw, under pressure resulting from his love for Emilia, a Gentile widow of good breeding, and his desire to keep her, Yasha decides to commit a robbery and promises to convert to Christianity, both acts inimical to his deepest, most basic instincts. The robbery is unsuccessful and he gives way to feelings of guilt and remorse growing out of the attempt, its aftermath, and his former promise to convert. In this, the second part of the novel, there occurs the supreme test of Yasha's attachment to Judaism and Jewish values.

The third and concluding section, the novel's epilogue, presents what may be described as the triumph of restraint and acceptance over the passion for freedom and unlimited knowledge, the renunciation of the life of sensual pleasure in favor of the way of life governed by Jewish Law and devotion to the holy books. For Yasha imposes upon himself an imprisonment designed for complete restraint and isolation, taking up residence in a cell "only four cubits long and four cubits wide," presumably to spend the remainder of his life there (224). Devoting his days to study of the Torah and repentance for past transgressions, Yasha becomes known as Reb Jacob the Penitent and acquires the reputation of being empowered to alleviate suffering, with the result that "he stood at his window from dawn until nightfall," receiving supplicants and giving advice and blessings (235). Thus Yasha's withdrawal from the world (unlike Rabbi Benish's in *Satan in Goray*) is consistent with the code of *mentshlekhkayt*, for, in receiving his fellow Jews in their time of trouble, Yasha remains involved with his fellow man and provides an important service to the community. Indeed, he is exalted in his isolation, for as the Lublin rabbi wrote, "He to whom Jews come in audience is a rabbi" (231).

Nevertheless, there is the paradox that even in his cell Yasha cannot completely avoid causing injury to others. As one example, his wife, Esther, "becomes in his penitence the deserted wife she never was throughout his many affairs."[21] Paradoxically, too, Yasha's imprisonment becomes a source of freedom for him, as it protects him from the burden of sensual temptations with which he remains afflicted in his cell, for "as long as he sat there, he was protected against the graver transgressions" (226). The cell itself is a kind of synagogue of Yasha's own making, and his confinement in it is the natural culmination of his relationship with the synagogue that develops throughout the book. An almost foreign place to Yasha at the novel's beginning, the synagogue becomes, by the end of the second part of the novel, his haven, his protection from his baser instincts and the consequences of his antisocial acts.

At the beginning of the novel Yasha is presented as an unconventional figure in the *shtetl*, who "wore no beard and went to synagogue only on Rosh Hashonah and Yom Kippur," and then only to please his wife, Esther. He

21. Cyrena N. Pondrom, "Conjuring Reality: I. B. Singer's *The Magician of Lublin*," in Allentuck, ed., *Achievement of Isaac Bashevis Singer*, p. 98.

"spent his Sabbath talking and smoking cigarettes among musicians," behavior which conveys the image of a *shtetl* nonconformist, of a man who values his freedom of action more than he does the observation of Jewish Law or his good reputation among his fellow ghetto dwellers (4). Beyond this nonconformity, Yasha has an air of mystery, almost of the supernatural, about him. This is partly, but only partly, attributable to his occupation as magician and his superhuman feats of daring and skill. This quality of mystery, in fact, has its origins to a large extent in his tumultuous state of mind, in the internal conflict between good and evil that is a feature of his daily existence. In consequence of his freedom of action Yasha had many mistresses, all of them dedicated to him. But although "he had sowed every variety of wild oats, had tangled and disentangled himself on numerous occasions," still "his marriage had remained sacred to him" (13). And in spite of the fact that "he had never concealed that he had a wife," his success in extramarital relationships was considerable.

Counterbalanced to Yasha's passion for self-indulgence is an instinct for restraint arising from his internalized standards of morality and his deep sense of responsibility to the Jewish community and identification with Jewish life. In short, his desires were harnessed by the *shtetl's* ethical code of *mentshlekhkayt*. Consequently the torments of hell raged within him, and he was a "soul searcher, prone to fantasy and strange conjecture" (12). "If the world had ever been informed of what went on inside of him, he, Yasha, would have long ago been committed to a madhouse" (14).

This internal moral struggle is reflected in Yasha's way of looking at the nature of the divine. Although he plays the nonbeliever with remarks such as "When were you in heaven, and what did God look like?," nevertheless he is not completely prepared to reject belief in God (4). Awestruck by the order in nature, Yasha sees the hand of God in evidence everywhere, in "each fruit blossom, pebble, and grain of sand" (6). "Oh, God Almighty, You are the magician, not I! . . . To bring out plants, flowers and colors from a bit of black soil!" (60). It is the precise *nature* of this God that remains a mystery to him, and he is consequently tormented by a host of unresolved questions: "What came after life? Was there such a thing as a soul? And what happened to it after it left the body? . . . He, himself, had experienced events unexplained by natural law, but what did it all mean?" (17). The result is that Yasha "was half Jew, half Gentile—neither Jew nor Gentile," with his own religious ideas: "There was a Creator, but He revealed Himself to no one, gave no indications of what was permitted or forbidden" (7).

Yasha's attitude toward God can be compared with his attitude toward his marriage: just as he treasures his wife and marriage, yet challenges them with his many love affairs, so also does Yasha maintain and treasure his belief in God, yet challenges him with his demand for proof of his existence and knowledge of his true nature. In spite of Yasha's mistresses and violations of Jewish Law, "he believed in only one God and one wife" (8).

In this questioning of the traditional beliefs of Judaism, in his assertion of the impossibility of fathoming God's true nature, Yasha separates himself from the Jewish community in Lublin, scoffing at the "pious certainty of believers," yet often envying their "unswerving faith." [22] His sense of isolation is revealed to us in the first scene in which Yasha comes in contact with a synagogue. He cannot un-

22. Buchen, p. 10.

derstand how Jews can speak to a God, deem "Him merci-
ful and compassionate," when only "plagues, famines, poverty, and pogroms were His gifts to them" (16). While
they had their God, Yasha had only doubt.

The dichotomy in Yasha's attitude toward traditional
Judaism is strikingly revealed by a comparison of his reaction to the Jews praying in the Lublin synagogue with the
second scene in which Yasha is confronted with a synagogue.
Somewhat confused by the rituals he observes in the synagogue ("Have I already forgotten so much of my heritage?"
(66)), Yasha is nevertheless drawn into its ambience, which
evokes memories of the past. He feels that everything, although "strangely foreign," is "yet familiar," that "he was
part of this community. Its roots were his roots. He bore its
mark upon his flesh. He understood the prayers" (66–67).
So overcome is Yasha by the feeling of intense Jewishness
that on his way out he kissess the *mezuzah* and takes with
him a torn prayer book. The mood continues at the inn
later that night; when observing the Jewish proprietors and
their young grandson he asks himself, "Can I forsake all
this? This is mine after all, mine. . . . Once I looked ex-
actly like that boy" (68–69). The atmosphere of the inn,
"alive with Sabbath, holidays, the anticipation of the Messiah, and of the world to come," touches Yasha deeply, and
we sense that he would be able to steal or convert to Christianity only with great difficulty, if at all, that such acts
would violate something very deep and essential in his nature (69).

Along with the synagogue, the images of the tightrope
and the lock are repeatedly associated with Yasha.[23] Both
represent the dualism of freedom and restraint which is an
important feature of Yasha's complex personality. Since the

23. Wolkenfeld discussess this point on pp. 355–358.

tightrope walker is able to walk high above the earth, he is free of the earth to which other, more ordinary mortals are bound. Yet since the rope itself must somehow be bound to the earth, so must the tightrope walker. It is in this sense that the tightrope represents Yasha's inner struggle between the desire for freedom of action and the restraint imposed by his moral code. One may think of the tightrope as the line dividing the world of earth-bound reality from the un-limited realm of the spirit, the supernatural world which is available to Yasha by virtue of his magic. In fact, Yasha lives and plays in both worlds, at some times without con-cern for virtue, at others with complete conscience. For although he was "ready to renounce his religion, yet—when he found a torn page from a holy book he always picked it up and put it to his lips" (58). Early in the novel Yasha has not yet found it necessary to choose between these two worlds, and the necessity is not forced upon him until the middle of the second part of the novel, when he attempts to carry through the robbery that is to provide the money for him to go off to Italy with Emilia.

Associated with the tightrope is the lock, which for or-dinary men is nothing but a symbol of restraint as it blocks their path, prevents their incursion. For Yasha, on the other hand, the lock represents freedom as well, since he can pick any lock in a matter of moments, a fact which makes the lock just another vehicle for the demonstration of his superior skills. It is not until the climactic scene in which Yasha fails miserably in an attempt to rob the house of Kazimierz Zaruski, a wealthy citizen of Warsaw, that Yasha finds the lock to be an impediment. In fact, during the attempt both the tightrope and the lock are suddenly transformed for the first time in Yasha's experience from symbols of freedom into symbols of restraint. Although the lock on Zaruski's safe "was obviously a neighborhood job, put together by an ordinary locksmith," Yasha fails to open it; furthermore, as he escapes from Zaruski's balcony, "his feet lacked their usual sureness," and he falls from the balcony's edge, causing a painful injury to his left foot (144). Yasha's skills with the lock and the rope, somehow linked together, leave him at the same critical moment in his life. With their loss he experiences as well the loss of his former sense of great freedom and power, a sense that had even led him to believe that one day he would be able to fly ("If a bird could do it, why not man? . . . He had drawers full of plans and diagrams. . . . What a sensation it would cause throughout the world if he, Yasha, flew over the rooftops of Warsaw or better still—Rome, Paris, or London" (38)), and he is forced to come to grips with the earthbound mortality he shares with all other men.

The humiliation of the theft scene is surprising on the face of it, in view of Yasha's earlier feats. However, we are given clues which, with hindsight, we may piece together to formulate an explanation. One set of indications centers about the shift in Yasha's personality, the loss of some of his self-confidence, whenever he arrives in Warsaw from Lublin. Although Yasha is attracted to the city and all his senses seem electrified by its congestion, its houses, palaces, shops, and cafés, nevertheless he loses the complete mastery that characterizes his presence in Lublin or Piask. This loss of mastery is reflected even in Yasha's relationship with women. Zeftel, Magda, and his own wife, Esther, all acquiesced to Yasha's demands, "neither capable nor desirous of opposition" (75). But in Warsaw, with Emilia, Yasha is the one controlled: "It was not he who had magnetized her, but the other way around" (21–22).

Other advance indications of Yasha's inability to com-

mit robbery (or a crime of any sort) center on his attachment to Jewish tradition and the code of *mentshlekhkayt,*
both in action and in thought and speech. A case in point
is Yasha's tender handling of Blind Mechl, whose carefully
constructed lock proves no match for the magician's ability.
For in respecting Blind Mechl's feelings, in being sensitive
to the danger of shaming him publicly, and in acting to
avoid this, Yasha is fulfilling an obligation imposed by the
moral code. It seems clear that Yasha's failure in his attempt at crime is guaranteed in advance by a combination
of innate honesty with loss of self-confidence. To the extent
that this failure is rooted in Yasha's respect for Jewish Law
("I still believe in the Eighth Commandment" (59)) and
his sense of continuity with the past ("He was descended
from people of honor" (84)), to that extent are we justified
in viewing the attempted robbery as a focal point in Yasha's
trial of Judaism and, in fact, as a vindication for Judaism in
this trial.

Another important focus for the trial of Judaism is Yasha's
promise to convert to Christianity. We see early in the
novel that his distaste for dogma and leaps of faith unsup-
ported by concrete evidence is not confined to Judaism. For
"the story of the immaculate conception and the explanation of the trinity—the Father, the Son, and the Holy
Ghost—seemed . . . even more unbelievable than the miracles the Hassidim attributed to their rabbis" (20). But
in a later scene when he is in the theater with Emilia,
"thoughts of repentance enveloped him. Perhaps there was
a God, after all? Perhaps all the holy sayings were true?"
(100). But this contemplated return to faith is short-lived
as Yasha once again reverts to his former skepticism concerning Judaism: "Where did it follow that the entire truth
was to be found in the Jewish codex? Maybe the answers lay

with the Christians, the Mohammedans, or still some other sect?" (100). This interplay of grasping for faith followed by a return to the old doubts remains a feature of Yasha's trial of Judaism throughout the novel, even in the final section, after his confinement to the cell.

To a large extent Yasha's testing of Judaism is enacted in his thoughts. The principal physical setting, however, is the synagogue, which takes on added significance in the light of its role as courtroom. Thus the trial on a conscious level really begins early in the first part of the novel, at the point when Yasha stops and glances in at the open door of the Lublin synagogue, revealing an alienation from Judaism for which we have already been prepared by his overt religious skepticism in the opening pages. The sense of alienation is shortly reinforced by Yasha's refusal to go to the synagogue for the Pentecost holiday, reasoning that "since God did not answer, why address Him?" (19). As we have observed, Yasha's second encounter with a synagogue presents a radically different view of his relationship to Judaism. Nevertheless, both scenes have in common a conflict of two opposing tendencies. The first synagogue scene, in which alienation predominates, still confronts Yasha with "something which he remembered from childhood"; in the second, in which Yasha finds himself drawn to the synagogue and the praying Jews, he finds the setting "strangely foreign" though familiar, and he refuses the opportunity to pray with the assembled congregation (16).

Yasha's third encounter with the synagogue, immediately after the failure of his attempt to rob Zaruski, develops the trial of Judaism still further. Although his skepticism reasserts itself, Yasha does not refuse the beadle's offer to "fetch [him] a prayer shawl and phylacteries," and for the first time in the novel he becomes part of a congregation of praying Jews (148). Observing Yasha's awkwardness in putting on the prayer shawl and phylacteries, the members of the congregation at first laugh at him but very soon begin to instruct him, drawing him into their midst. It has been a long time since Yasha has prayed, but one of the congregation observes that "it is never too late," and the Jews, "who but a moment before had watched him with a sort of adult derision, now looked upon him with curiosity, respect, and affection" (150). The palpable sense of community, the response to the code of *mentshlekhkayt* on the part of his fellow Jews of the congregation, is not lost on Yasha. He "distinctly sensed the love which flowed from their persons to him," and he felt shame "because he had betrayed this fraternity, befouled it, stood ready to cast it aside" (151).

Yasha, recalling that he is "descended from generations of God-fearing Jews," is drawn to his past, his tradition, and returns to the community of Jews, never again to be parted from it. He now feels his skepticism slip away: "God had created the world. He does have compassion for His creatures. He does reward those who fear Him" (151). And he is struck by the true cause of his failure to carry through the scheme to run off with Emilia: "It was obvious that those in heaven did not intend to have him turn to crime, desert Esther, convert" (152). Yasha is overcome by a return to faith, "a faith that demanded no proof, an awe of God, a sense of remorse over one's transgressions" (152–153). He is thankful to be standing "in prayer shawl and phylacteries, prayer book in hand, amongst a group of honest Jews" (152). The scene ends with Yasha's resolution to be a Jew, "a Jew like all the others!" This vow assumes importance "because it represents not a recognition of self-identity but the acceptance of moral obligation to act in a certain way." [24]

24. Pondrom, "Conjuring Reality," p. 105.

However, this commitment is challenged, for upon his departure from the synagogue God is once again on trial as Yasha, in the ancient Jewish tradition, challenges him directly: "If You want me to serve you, Oh God, reveal Yourself, perform a miracle, let Your voice be heard, give me some sign . . ." (155). His decision to "become a real synagogue Jew" does not eliminate his struggle between faith and skepticism. Here Yasha glimpses what for him is to be the ultimate solution: the necessity to live with self-imposed discipline, the need for the restraints of man-made dogma in spite of the absence of unquestioning faith in God. Living life according to Jewish Law and *mentshlekhkayt* is desirable independently of the nature of faith professed.

The third section of the novel (the epilogue) finds Yasha back in Lublin with Esther three years later; at this point he has been doing penance in his small brick cell for more than a year. For the first year and a half after his return he studied and absorbed vast amounts of the Torah for the sole purpose of discussing with the Lublin rabbi the theologically delicate question of isolation from the world as a means of repentance. Yasha "produced for the Rabbi a variety of prototypes—saints who had had themselves put under restraint for fear they would be unable to resist temptation. . . . Harsh laws were merely fences to restrain a man from sin" (223). Unable to sway Yasha in his resolve to withdraw from the community, "the Rabbi had placed his hand upon Yasha's head and had blessed him [saying], 'Your actions are intended for the glory of Heaven. May the Almighty help you!'" (223).

In the epilogue Yasha's trial of Judaism continues, but on the level of *faith* only, the question of Yasha's action having already been resolved with his confinement. Thus *The Magician of Lublin* "is not the story of conversion from doubt to faith, nor from one kind of faith to another," but, on the other hand, "while faith does not change in the novel, action does."[25] Although Yasha's challenge to God goes on, he has made a commitment to a life consonant with the code of *mentshlekhkayt*, a life ruled by Jewish Law, and he honors that commitment, regardless of his continuing doubts on the theological level. And this is precisely what is intrinsically Jewish in Yasha's conversion, that faith is viewed as less significant than deed, that lack of faith is far overshadowed by right action (in the sense of Jewish Law).[26] In spite of Singer's comment on Yasha's imprisonment—"according to Jewish religion this is not a way of salvaging your soul . . ."—we may conclude that Yasha's reputation as a holy man is not meant in an ironic sense.[27] For Singer has also said: ". . . if we break the Ten Commandments, we are really in great trouble. . . . I think that the Ten Commandments contain the greatest human wisdom; the question is only how to keep them. And also the question is, is it possible to keep them?"[28] In advising his supplicants to "harm no one. Slander no one. Not even think evil," and in adhering to his own advice, Yasha fulfills an obligation to God and man, even in his confinement, by advancing the cause of the decent life, lived in accordance with the Ten Commandments (237). Thus, while the trial of faith continues at the end of the novel, Judaism as a way of life is vindicated. In Yasha's imaginary debate

25. *Ibid.*, pp. 95–96.
26. The Jewish tradition allows a man to be an atheist, yet at the same time a "good Jew" because of his just action and adherence to the Law. "He who transacts his business honestly and is pleasing to his fellow men is accounted as having fulfilled the entire Torah." See S. S. Cohon, *Judaism: A Way of Life* (New York, 1962), p. 102.
27. Cyrena N. Pondrom, "Isaac Bashevis Singer: An Interview, Part I," *Contemporary Literature*, X (Winter, 1969), 9.
28. *Ibid.*, pp. 11–12.

with Satan, he hypothesizes "for the sake of argument . . . that God does not exist, but that the words spoken in His name are nevertheless correct" (229). Yasha's conclusion from this hypothesis, summarizing his final position, is nothing less than a reinterpretation of the covenant itself: "If there is no God, man must behave like God."

THREE

The Holocaust: Nelly Sachs
and André Schwarz-Bart

The Jewish catastrophe in Europe, the complete
destruction of Singer's *shtetl* and the consequent demise of
the *shtetl* culture, has given rise to a large number of literary
works, collectively referred to as literature of the holocaust,
in a variety of genres, of greatly varying literary value, and
written in several languages. Almost all of these works, independent of their literary value, are of some historical
interest, as the overwhelming majority of them have been
written by survivors, eyewitnesses to the tragedy and victims of it. This is indeed the source of the very personal
quality and power to move the reader that most of this
literature possesses. Many of the survivors who have written of the holocaust have done so primarily with one purpose in mind—to bear witness, to testify to the occurrence
of these unbelievable events, so that the world might eventually come to accept their truth, even if it could never
fathom their real meaning, if indeed there is a meaning
separate from the events themselves.[1] These are the literary
amateurs, those who have felt the need to write about the
events of their past only because of the enormity of those

1. Elie Wiesel has said, "To me, the holocaust teaches nothing."
See "Jewish Values in the Post-Holocaust Future," *Judaism*, XVI
(Summer, 1967), 287.

events. There are others, writers of great talent and power such as André Schwartz-Bart, Elie Wiesel, and Nelly Sachs, who might have written in any case but because of their personal involvement have turned their literary talents to discussions of the holocaust and its implications for mankind.

Nelly Sachs, Schwarz-Bart, and Wiesel, in their separate ways, share as a major concern of their work the questions of the continued viability of Judaism and the justice of God in the light of the holocaust and its aftermath. A closely related concern is the interplay between the trial of Judaism and accusation against God on the one hand and the ethical code of *mentshlekhkayt* on the other. We have previously pointed out that the code of *mentshlekhkayt* deals primarily with the problem of how a good man ought to live. Incredibly, under the conditions of the holocaust, the code did not become inoperative but, rather, was adapted to address a problem even more basic: how a man can retain his essential humanity. Eugene Heimler, for example, in *Night of the Mist*, asks, "Tell me, on what does it depend whether a man remains a man?" [2] Many other writers of the holocaust deal with various aspects and ramifications of this same question, some asserting the possibility of remaining human under inhuman conditions, and a few, like the psychiatrist Viktor Frankl, even describing their methods of doing so.[3]

Many of the literary works that have emerged from the holocaust (including diaries and nonliterary or quasi-literary eyewitness accounts) share these concerns to a greater or

2. Eugene Heimler, *Night of the Mist* (New York, 1959), p. 128.

3. Viktor E. Frankl, *Man's Search for Meaning* (New York, 1969).

lesser degree, and thus the biblical figure of Job is often prominently mentioned, especially in connection with rebellion against God. As Wiesel has pointed out, "The Book of Job: that tale was in high style then, every survivor of the holocaust could have written it." [4] The treatment of Job affords some insight into the various attitudes toward Jewish tradition that arise within the body of holocaust literature. Eliezer, the young protagonist of Wiesel's *Night*, imprisoned in Auschwitz, cries out: "How I sympathized with Job! I did not deny God's existence, but I doubted His absolute justice" (53).[5] Wiesel's use of Job to express man's challenge to God contrasts with the aspect of Job emphasized by Nelly Sachs in her choice of epigraph to "O die Schornsteine" from the poetry collection *In den Wohnungen des Todes:* "And when this, my skin, will be destroyed, I shall gaze upon God without my flesh" (Job 19:26).[6] This emphasis upon Job's allegiance to God in spite of his great suffering is entirely consistent with Miss Sachs's declared purpose of reconciliation of the holocaust with traditional Jewish beliefs and, in particular, with the traditional Jewish view of God: "Always intent upon raising the unspeakable to a transcendental plane, in *order to make it tolerable.* . . ." [7] The process of reconciliation is actually nothing other than an oblique form of the trial of Judaism. To be sure, the trial is less overt than, for example, in

4. Elie Wiesel, *Legends of Our Time* (New York, 1968), p. 97.
5. Elie Wiesel, *Night* (New York, 1960).
6. Nelly Sachs, *In den Wohnungen des Todes,* in the collection *Fahrt ins Staublose: Die Gedichte der Nelly Sachs* (Frankfurt am Main, 1961), p. 8; translation mine.
7. *Ibid.* See Nelly Sachs, "Eli, Ein Mysterienspiel vom Leiden Israels" in *Zeichen im Sand: Die szenischen Dichtungen der Nelly Sachs* (Frankfurt am Main, 1962), Notes, p. 345; italics and translation mine.

Wiesel, where direct accusations are made against God. Nevertheless, in Nelly Sachs's poetic drama *Eli* reconciliation entails an examination of the assumptions of Judaism, in particular testing the power of prayer against the forces of cruelty; to the extent that it does so, *Eli* carries out a trial of Judaism. In the end, as we shall see, Miss Sachs resolves the trial in favor of Judaism, affirming her belief in the power of prayer to overcome evil, the power of faith to overcome destruction. This affirmation may well be the principal aim of her art, the principal underpinning of her aesthetics.

This position of Nelly Sachs stands in opposition to that expressed by Wiesel, whose attitude toward the Jewish experience has been shaped by his early intense preoccupation with Judaism in the *shtetl* in which he was brought up and tempered by years in Nazi concentration camps: "I believe that God *is* part of our experience. The Jew, in my view, may rise against God, provided he remains within God. One can be a very good Jew, observe all the *mitzvot*, study Talmud—and yet be against God." [8] The relationship with Judaism enunciated here by Wiesel exemplifies the observation of Harold Schulweis that "the tone of rebellion in Jewish literature is authentic. It is not considered blasphemous: indeed, it is canonized. The indignation rises from within the religious framework, not from without. . . . Out of personal anguish, the sufferer questions, cries out, defies but does not deny." [9]

Where Wiesel admits his inability to reconcile God with

8. Wiesel, "Jewish Values," p. 299.
9. Harold Schulweis, "Man and God: The Moral Partnership," in *Jewish Heritage Reader* (New York, 1968), p. 120. Wiesel fits Schulweis's thesis so precisely that one might surmise that the latter wrote with Wiesel in mind. In fact, his article does not mention Wiesel, drawing mainly upon biblical and other classical sources.

the holocaust and ends by conceding the presence of evil in God,[10] Nelly Sachs achieves a resolution by adopting the position, in the tradition of the Book of Isaiah, that during the holocaust God turned away from his people and was in hiding.[11] With the solution of one problem, another arises, that of bringing God back among his people. Here again the efficacy of prayer is challenged, this time with respect to its power to force God from his place of hiding. *Eli* is to a large extent a plea for the survivors of the holocaust to "re-establish their relationship to God and to regain his attention—in effect to bring him out of hiding," and an examination of the thesis that through prayer this can, in fact, be accomplished.[12] Unspeakable evil is everywhere in *Eli*, yet Nelly Sachs attempts to delineate within that evil the contours of God and goodness. This accounts in part for the interplay in *Eli* between hope and despair, between a sense of rebirth, of the reawakening of life, and the presence of death. Written in 1943, shortly after Miss Sachs's escape to Sweden from Berlin, *Eli* is projected forward in time to the period immediately following the holocaust. A number of Jewish survivors have come together to begin life anew and to rebuild their town out of the rubble of the old one. At the same time preparations are being made to celebrate the Jewish New Year, Rosh Hashana. The juxtaposition of the remnants of life against the celebration which affirms life raises the questions: How can

10. Byron L. Sherwin, "Elie Wiesel and Jewish Theology," *Judaism*, XVIII (Winter, 1969), 46. See also Elie Wiesel, *The Gates of the Forest* (New York, 1966), pp. 196–197.

11. David Bronsen, "The Dead among the Living: Nelly Sachs' Eli," *Judaism*, XVI (Winter, 1967), 124. See *Isaiah* 45:15: "Verily, thou art a God that hidest thyself, O God of Israel, the Saviour."

12. Bronsen, p. 124.

these survivors celebrate the New Year? For what have
they to be thankful?

In the tradition of the Expressionist drama, several of the
characters tell of particular events which they cannot erase
from their minds. The Washerwoman tells how eight-year-
old Eli was murdered: "And when Eli saw, / . . . how
they drove his parents through the Cattle Lane, . . . / . . .
he put the pipe to his mouth and blew it. / . . . He pointed
the pipe to Heaven, / he piped to God . . ." (315). She
continues to tell of how a soldier marching with the herded
captives "looked around and saw Eli / piping to high
heaven / [and] struck him down dead with his rifle butt"
(314–315).[13] Nor can the Bakerwoman deaden the sound
of her dead husband's footsteps that throb in her head.
Yet the pipelayer, Samuel, the grandfather of Eli, who was
struck dumb when he witnessed the child's death, continues to lay pipes at the fountain so that it may flow
for Rosh Hashana. And by the end of this opening scene
the fountain does begin to run, and both the Washerwoman and the Bakerwoman rejoice at this first indication
of reawakening life. At this moment the Bakerwoman cups
her hands and drinks from the fountain in the hope that
the water will drown out the pounding of the footsteps in
her ears. The life symbolism of the fountain is thus mixed
with reminders of death. At the beginning of the process
of rebirth Miss Sachs does not let us forget the holocaust.
It is as if she is insisting, in response to the code of *mentshlekhkayt*, that life must go on, but at the same time ac-
knowledging the difficulty of overcoming the reminders of
overwhelming evil to achieve the triumph of life over death.

The second scene of the play shows us the marketplace

13. Nelly Sachs, *Eli*, in *O the Chimneys* (New York, 1967).
Further page references, to this edition, will appear in the text.

from a different angle. The fountain still runs, the old synagogue is gone, and in its place a prayer tent has been set up. Surrounding the whole scene is green landscape. In the rubble are found bits of colored ribbon, a skull cap, a prayer shawl. The drama continues to move in the direction of the contemplation of evil. "Nerves grown perpetually anguished by too much suffering cannot tolerate seemingly harmless incidents because they summon up unbearable associations." [14] Thus the widow of the stonemason, having lost her child and also her husband, who died of over-work in a stone quarry, is unable to bear the stones which are to be the building material of the new house. She reacts by recreating "her child out of air" and killing herself, smashing her forehead against the stones (321). Once again it seems impossible to begin life anew amidst such suffering; the tenets of Judaism, the code of *mentsh-lekhkayt*, seem inappropriate, inapplicable; the expectation that these survivors can once again be *mentshen* appears unfounded. Yet in spite of the sorrow that surrounds him, in spite of evidences and remnants of his murdered people, the Bricklayer continues to sing and whistle, asserting life and his own *mentshlekhkayt*, not merely as a possibility but rather as a necessity under these circumstances: "Don't cry, Jossele. / Let us build the old house anew. / If tears hang on the stonework, / if sighs hang on the woodwork, / if the little children can't sleep, / death has a soft bed" (322). The scene ends on this hopeful sign with the Brick-layer trying to establish contact with God.

Later we are given further symbols of hope, of rebirth and regeneration. A young woman, in spite of the times, has managed to bear and nurse a child. At the close of Scene Six all of the unfortunate survivors "are as if blotted out by the glare of the evening sun," leaving only the young

14. Bronsen, p. 121.

woman with her child visible in the light (338). This op-
timistic turning toward the future and away from the past
is continued several scenes later, on the eve of Rosh
Hashana, when the worshippers repeatedly express the belief that their prayers are taking wing toward heaven. The
following Scene Nine continues to emphasize the symbolism of hope and the reawakening of life. The fountain has
continued to run, and as the young bricklayers pass toward their work of rebuilding the town, they fill their jugs
with water. One of the bricklayers speaks of marriage to a
girl standing nearby, and they all express determination to
build a new life.

Stark contrast is afforded in Scene Eleven, which opens
with a Voice from the Chimney: "We stones were the
last things to touch Israel's sorrow. / Jeremiah's body in
smoke, / Job's body in smoke, / the Lamentations in smoke,
/ whimpering of little children in smoke, / mother's cradle
songs in smoke, / Israel's way of freedom in smoke" (363).
This scene presents the confrontation of Hirsch, the tailor,
with death. Describing how he was forced to cremate his
own people, Hirsch declares that as he did so, he cremated
God as well. Then, in an act of desperation, he throws his
prayer shawl into the smoke of the chimney in the crema-
torium. When the shawl touches the smoke, the chimney
begins to crumble, and a Giant Form, wrapping itself in
the prayer shawl, rises into the sky, singing the *Shema*,
the traditional Hebrew prayer celebrating the uniqueness
of God: "Hear, O Israel / He our God, / He the One"
(366).[15] At this point the dying Hirsch falls to the ground,
he too reciting the *Shema*. The incident suggests that,

15. Miss Sachs renders the *Shema* in German rather than in the
original Hebrew. Bronsen, discussing this point, pp. 127–128, argues
that it must be so rendered, and views this circumstance as a feature of Miss Sachs's "German-Jewish symbiosis."

through prayer, man must strive to remain strong, withstand suffering, and perhaps help God emerge from the eclipse into which he was thrown during the holocaust. In remaining faithful to God in the face of atrocity, Hirsh reflects Miss Sachs's emphasis upon Job's acceptance of God rather than his challenge to God.

In the play's final scene, Michael, who, Miss Sachs points out, is one of the thirty-six Just Men, one of the *Lamed-Vov Zaddikim*, whose existence justifies Mankind, comes face to face with the soldier who bludgeoned Eli to death. The soldier's child has died, suffering over some nameless loss, like Eli an innocent victim of evil. "In this dismal world," Miss Sachs has said, "innocence always becomes the victim." [16] The two children in their suffering provide a human link between victim and executioner. Now, confronted by Michael, the murderer begins to shout and shriek, and then "the murderer disintegrates into dust at the countenance of Michael, which radiates divine splendor (picture of peace)." [17] Thus the drama ends on a note of retribution and with the hope that Eli's death will have been the last earthly suffering for the Jews. In confronting death with prayer, Miss Sachs's characters put Judaism on trial, testing its power to support hope and life in the face of the ultimate evil. *Eli* expresses the view that, despite the existence of evil, prayer can and must continue, and, beyond this, the faith that prayer is a sustaining force which can repeatedly overcome evil. Thus Judaism proves capable of withstanding evil and is thereby vindicated in its trial.

The power of faith and prayer to overcome evil and renew the world is explicitly mentioned by Nelly Sachs in

16. See Sachs, "Eli," in *Zeichen im Sand*, Notes, p. 344; translation mine.

17. *Ibid.*

the notes to *Beryll sieht in der Nacht*: "Beryll is one of the Thirty-six, whose fervor in enduring *begins the world anew, again and again*." [18] The Beryll of *Eli* is Michael, who is thought by the survivors to be one of the thirty-six Just Men. According to Bronsen, God continues to exist in *Eli*, "and the structure of His law is still operative in the person of Michael." [19] In fact, much of the work of Nelly Sachs reflects a preoccupation with the legend of the *Lamed-Vov*, which, not surprisingly, is widely present in Jewish literature of the holocaust.

In this connection it is useful to consider André Schwarz-Bart's *The Last of the Just*, in which the legend is elevated to the status of a central, unifying theme, the leitmotif of the novel. Schwarz-Bart renders the legend of the Just Men early in his work: "The world reposes on thirty-six Just Men, the *Lamed-Vov*, indistinguishable from simple mortals; often they are unaware of their station. But if one of them were lacking, the sufferings of mankind would poison even the souls of the newborn, and humanity would suffocate with a single cry" (4–5).[20] Ernie Levy, the protagonist of this work, is one of the *Lamed-Vov*, a fact of central importance to his role as a human being and to any meaningful grasp of the complexities of his character. Schwarz-Bart begins "the true history of Ernie Levy" not with Ernie himself but rather with his ancestor Rabbi Yom Tov Levy, who was martyred by his own hand during a pogrom in York in the year 1185. One of the few survivors is his infant son, Solomon, who is to become the first *Lamed-Vovnik* of his family.

18. See Nelly Sachs, "Beryll," in *Zeichen im Sand*, Notes, p. 353; translation and italics mine.
19. Bronsen, p. 124.
20. André Schwarz-Bart, *The Last of the Just* (New York, 1960).

The question of the nature of God's justice and the reality of the purpose of the Just Men becomes detailed with the life of Mordecai Levy, the grandfather of Ernie Levy. For Mordecai, the purpose of the *Lamed-Vov* is clear. He "takes our suffering upon himself . . . and raises it to Heaven and sets it at the feet of the Lord—who forgives. Which is why the world goes on . . . in spite of our sins" (57). Yet when he thinks of the wickedness of the world into which his child is to be born, he wonders about the justice of God: "He could think only of the cold, the hunger, the blue sickness. . . . Does God . . . wish the death of infants?" (61). But Mordecai comes to a decision. He will trust God. Like Wiesel's characters, Benjamin, the child of Mordecai, cannot so easily justify the ways of God. He considers the words of an old tailor who no longer believes in God because there is no longer any reason to. Benjamin tries to visualize the world through this old man's eyes and suddenly it comes to him that all the suffering "goes for nothing" (69).

Later Benjamin encounters Yankel, a young Jew who, as the sole survivor of a pogrom, had to bury his whole village after it was over. Yankel, no longer able to believe in God, asks the question: "What can a Jew do, who is no longer a Jew, to avoid spending his life on all fours?" His answer: "You want to make a calf of me, I'll become a butcher!" (94). Yankel is referring here to a loss of *mentshlekhkayt*. The Jew is caught in the paradox that if he is to remain a man, to survive at a level beyond that of an animal, he must become a killer and thus violate his own moral code. Like Yankel, Benjamin can no longer find the strength to believe. He too has lived through World War I, pogroms, senseless slaughter. He tells his father that he no longer believes in the history of the *Lamed-Vov*.

Thus Ernie Levy, descendant of Solomon Levy, son of Benjamin and grandson of Mordecai, born in the second quarter of the twentieth century, inherits two diametrically opposed positions, that of his father, Benjamin, and that of his grandfather, Mordecai. Ernie's grandfather instructs him in the essential function of the *Lamed-Vovnik*: "He senses all the evil in the land, and takes it to his heart!" (166). That is, the outstanding characteristic of the *Lamed-Vovnik* is the degree to which he practices the code of *mentshlekhkayt*. The connection with the ethical code is revealed, for example, in Ernie's question, "What should a Just Man do in this life?" (166). In essence, he is here asking to know the attributes of *mentshlekhkayt* and how they can best be fulfilled. Already as a young child Ernie is deeply concerned with the possibilities of improving man's lot in the world. Responding to his grandfather's explanation of the Just Man's role, Ernie expresses dissatisfaction at the mere apprehension of evil: "But what good does it do to sense [evil] if nothing is changed?" (174). To the grandfather's reply, "It changes for God," Ernie in turn responds once more: "If it's only for God, then I don't understand anything." He concludes that if God asks the Germans to persecute the Jews, then the Jews must "have done something to [God], otherwise he wouldn't be angry at us that way, at just us, the Jews" (174). With this scene Ernie's trial of Judaism has begun.

In Ernie's case the trial of Judaism takes the shape of loss of faith, but not so much in God as in *mentshlekhkayt* and the possibility of living in the world as a good Jew. *"To be a Jew is impossible,"* his father had told him, and now he comes to agree (279). The argument that the persecution of the Jews somehow serves God's higher purposes, that the Jews are "the tribute of suffering that man

. . . offers to God," had not impressed Benjamin Levy, and it does not now impress his son (267). The loss of faith is mixed with feelings of shame and guilt, for Ernie reasons that there must be some underlying cause for the historical persecution of the Jews. For Ernie the guilt attaches not merely to the Jews as a people but to himself, personally, as well: *"I was not a Just Man, I was nothing"* (242).

The trial of Judaism reaches a critical stage when Ernie learns that his family has been taken to a Nazi extermination camp. "If it is the will of the Eternal, our God, I damn his name and beg him to gather me up close enough to spit in his face" (285). This bitter, direct accusation of God is in the tradition of Job and, as in Job, Ernie displays no inclination whatever to deny the existence of God, only his justice. The nadir of Ernie's crisis is reached following the death of his family. Consumed in Jewish self-hatred, Ernie assumes the guise of a Gentile and resolves to turn himself into a dog. He "cultivates his lowest instincts in an attempt to subvert and disfigure his humanity," perhaps in defiance of God and as an act of revenge against him.[21] When he is recognized as a Jew (". . . I couldn't see your face very well, but . . . I *recognized your eyes*" (299)), Ernie himself has a moment of recognition, realizing the baseness of his attempt to deny his Jewishness; he is brought to the point of utter despair. From this point of complete hopelessness, Ernie then begins to achieve a reintegration into life. He rejoins his people not only in spirit but physically as well, traveling to occupied Paris and joining the Jewish community there. Afterward he voluntarily enters the Drancy concentration

21. Judah Pilch, *The Jewish Catastrophe in Europe* (New York, 1968), p. 195.

camp and is ultimately transported with his fellow Jews to Auschwitz and death. Although Ernie could easily have avoided this fate by continuing to pose as a Gentile, he refuses to do so. Ernie Levy has accepted his role as Jew and as *Lamed-Vovnik*, and never again does he separate himself from the Jewish people. At the end of the novel we are left with the feeling that for man to be able to survive, assimilating the knowledge of evil, God is a necessity. God provides the final triumph of the victims over the executioners. Near the end of the work, in a freight car on the way to Auschwitz, Ernie talks to the children about the Kingdom of Israel, where it is beautiful and warm, an enchanted land, so he says, to which they are going. In doing this, he really is speaking metaphorically of the ultimate triumph of good over evil.

As he lies dying in the gas chamber, Ernie remembers the legend of Rabbi Chanina ben Teradion. Wrapped in the scrolls of the Torah and flung upon the pyre by the Romans for having taught the Law, the Rabbi was asked by a pupil what he saw. " 'I see the parchment burning, but the letters are taking wing' " (374). In this legend there is affirmation of life, a difficult affirmation to be sure, but affirmation nonetheless. Judaism, having been put on trial, is vindicated because, through the code of *mentshlekhkayt*, it reveres and affirms life under any and all conditions. The fear of Benjamin Levy that all the suffering "goes for nothing" has proved unfounded.

FOUR

The Holocaust: Elie Wiesel

In the work of Elie Wiesel, even more than in that of Nelly Sachs or André Schwartz-Bart, the trial of Judaism and God achieves the status of a theme of central, perhaps overriding importance, as it is expounded, amplified, and developed throughout his first five novels. In the concentration camp Buna, against the background of Eliezer's earlier deep reverence for God and profound commitment to Judaism, not merely as a religious system but rather as a way of life, the antithetical accusation against God is interposed: "This day I had ceased to plead. I was no longer capable of lamentation. On the contrary, I felt very strong. I was the accuser, God the accused" (73).[1]

Byron Sherwin has pointed out that Wiesel's blasphemy is "firmly within a tradition which finds its sources in Biblical theology and which develops throughout Jewish literature, notably Cabbalistic writings." [2] Sherwin develops this point of view to the conclusion that, far from removing himself from Judaism and Jewish life, Wiesel is one of "those reconstructionists of faith who have arisen amongst traditional Jewish blasphemers after each major tragedy in Jewish history." [3] This view is supported by Wiesel himself

1. Elie Wiesel, *Night* (New York, 1960).
2. Byron L. Sherwin, "Elie Wiesel and Jewish Theology, *Judaism*, XVIII (Winter, 1969), 40.
3. *Ibid.*

in asserting the possibility of being, simultaneously, a "very good Jew" and "yet against God." There is, in fact, no suggestion in Wiesel of a rejection of the *idea* of God, of any possible suspension in the belief in God's existence, but rather the assertion that God has sinned against man. When Wiesel speaks in apparent contradiction of rising "against God" while remaining "within God," he is suggesting that the Jew continue to uphold his part of Israel's ancient covenant with God, even while recognizing that God has not upheld his side and rebuking him accordingly. The covenant explains Wiesel's apparent contradiction and, simultaneously, "the extraordinary intimacy and audacity allowable within the relationship between Israel and the deity," [4] well documented in Talmudic commentaries and the Mosaic Testament itself. This intimate, audacious aspect of classical Jewish writings finds its counterpart in Wiesel's novels, among which his fifth novel, *The Gates of the Forest*, may be taken as representative, since it summarizes and develops further the major themes present in the first four.

The Gates of the Forest begins with an intriguing parable concerning the Rabbi Israel Baal Shem-Tov, founder of Hasidism, and his followers: "When the great Rabbi Israel Baal Shem-Tov saw misfortune threatening the Jews it was his custom to go into a certain part of the forest to meditate. There he would light a fire, say a special prayer, and the miracle would be accomplished and the misfortune averted" (Introduction).[5] His disciple, the Magid of Mezritch, could accomplish the miracle even though he did not know how to light the fire; later Rabbi Moshe-Leib of

4. Harold Schulweis, "Man and God: The Moral Partnership," in *Jewish Heritage Reader* (New York, 1968), p. 121.
5. Elie Wiesel, *The Gates of the Forest* (New York, 1966).

Sasov, having forgotten both the prayer and how to light the fire, could still save his people by merely knowing the place. In the final section of the parable, when it fell to Rabbi Israel of Rizhyn to overcome misfortune, even the place had been forgotten: "I am unable to light the fire and I do not know the prayer; I cannot even find the place in the forest. All I can do is to tell the story, and this must be sufficient. And it was sufficient" (Introduction).

The parable is important in several respects. In the first place it foreshadows the preoccupation of the novel with the possibilities of Hasidic mysticism as a viable way of life for man after the horrors of Auschwitz, and especially for the survivors of those horrors. Second, it suggests that the answer to the gnawing question of what a survivor can do in the face of the holocaust, to defy the torturers and perhaps to avert future catastrophes, may be simply to continue to survive and bear witness: "All I can do is to tell the story, and this must be sufficient" (Introduction). On one occasion at least Wiesel has made this point explicitly: "During the war, some Jews attempted to escape and to survive for one reason only: to tell the story. . . . For deep down people lived and died in fear: perhaps the last Jew will disappear, and the tale will die with him." [6] The final line of the parable is a suggestion of the hope present in this novel, a hope totally absent from *Night*, and to be found in the succeeding novels, *Dawn*, *The Accident*, and *The Town beyond the Wall*, only in slowly increasing measure. Having lost all hope and rejected Talmudic Judaism in *Night*, Wiesel gradually comes to discover new hope within the tradition of Hasidic Judaism.

This gradual change is intimately connected with the

6. Elie Wiesel, "Jewish Values in the Post-Holocaust Future," *Judaism*, XVI (Summer, 1967), 283.

trial of Judaism in Wiesel's work. Faced with the enormities of the German concentration camp in *Night*, the
young protagonist rejects Judaism and its God completely
and, he believes, forever: "Never shall I forget those flames
which consumed my faith forever. . . . Never shall I forget those moments which murdered my God and my soul"
(45). To the young Eliezer the evidence is overwhelming,
the verdict in the trial is a foregone conclusion. In contrast,
well after the war's end and toward the end of *The Gates
of the Forest*, the protagonist (now called Gregor), still
putting God and Judaism on trial, still suffering from the
effects of the holocaust, hears evidence for Judaism's defense (if not for God's) in his conversation with the
Hasidic rebbe in Brooklyn. Against Gregor's indictment of
God, the rebbe brings to bear Hasidic affirmation of the
joy in life: "There is joy as well as fury in the *hasid*'s danc-
ing. It's his way of proclaiming, 'You don't want me to
dance; too bad, I'll dance anyhow. You've taken away every
reason for singing, but I shall sing. . . . Yes, my joy will
rise up; it will submerge you'" (196). The earlier total rejection has at this point come to seem simplistic and unacceptable, and the trial of Judaism begins now to reach a
new level of development. As is the case with the protagonists of Eugene Heimler and Nelly Sachs, Gregor is
possessed by the need, at long last, to turn his back upon
the holocaust and rejoin the living. This need forces him
to re-examine Judaism and seek a viable existence within
Jewish tradition.

The final scene of *The Gates of the Forest* finds Gregor
reverting to his original Jewish name, Gavriel, and reciting
the *Kaddish*, the traditional prayer for the dead, in the
Hasidic synagogue. This scene represents a reaffirmation
and strengthening of the hope Gregor found in his con-

versation with the rebbe. In agreeing to the request of the young Yeshiva boy that he join the nine waiting men to form the complete *Minyan* of ten required for a prayer service, Gregor/Gavriel is responding to the sense of community which forms one of the basic tenets of the code of *mentshlekhkayt*. In reciting the *Kaddish* with the *Minyan*, he begins to re-establish his faith in life and his relation to the Jewish community and Jewish tradition. This, we are allowed to hope, is the first important step in Gregor's return to the community of man. For the *Kaddish* is dedicated to the dead but contains no reference at all to death. It is, in a real sense, a prayer devoted to the support of the living survivors, that they, in reciting it, may draw comfort from the Jewish community, represented in this case by the congregation. We recognize in this assignment of priorities, in this recognition that the living rather than the dead need our sympathy and support, a point of view completely consistent with the principal emphasis of the code of *mentshlekhkayt*.

The act of reciting the *Kaddish* does not, per se, mark a turning point for Gregor, for he has in fact recited it every year upon the anniversary of his father's death. But, in contrast to the final scene in the novel, he has done this only out of the inertia of tradition, because it "conformed to the custom of countless generations of sages and orphans" (7).[7] It has been an act of resignation rather than an expression of faith in life or of the will to go on: ". . . I shall go to the synagogue. . . . I will light the candles, I will say *Kaddish*, and it will be for me further proof of my impotence" (*Legends*, 7). Even the indifference expressed here had marked a change from the still earlier refusal to recite the *Kaddish*, because "there was nothing more to

7. Elie Wiesel, *Legends of Our Time* (New York, 1968).

say, nothing more to hope for" (*Legends,* 3). Not only is Jewish Law rejected here, but likewise the tradition of the code of *mentshlekhkayt,* which does not concede the possibility of "nothing more to hope for."

By the time of his father's death, Eliezer had long since turned his back on his earlier dedication to the Talmud: "The student of the Talmud, the child that I was, had been consumed in the flames" (*Night,* 46). Eliezer, never doubting God's existence, doubting rather his power and absolute justice, addresses him repeatedly in accusing tones: "Who are you, my God . . . compared to this afflicted crowd. . . . What does Your greatness mean . . . in the face of all this weakness, this decomposition, this decay?" (75). As in Nelly Sachs's *Eli,* there is no sense in Wiesel's works that God is dead; rather, he dies over and over again: "Where is God now? Where is He? Here He is—He is hanging here on this gallows . . ." (74). God is sometimes addressed ironically, as when the mud covers Eliezer's new shoes, making it possible for him to keep them: "I thanked God, in an improvised prayer, for having created mud in His infinite and marvelous universe" (47). More often there is direct and bitter accusation: "Why, but why should I bless Him? [He] who chose us from among the races to be tortured day and night, to see our fathers, our mothers, our brothers, end in the crematory? . . . Who hast chosen us to be butchered on thine altar?" (73). Eliezer quickly reaches the point where he is convinced that God, with his silence in the face of absolute evil, is guilty, and as "an act of revolt and of rebellion against Him" decides not to fast on Yom Kippur (75). In view of the boy's background of deeply religious fervor, this is a major decision of crucial emotional import. Eliezer can no longer accept God's silence, and the reaction is all the stronger for his not having lost faith in God's existence. He does not become an atheist or an agnostic; he remains a Jew, but a Jew who has repudiated the Jewish God.

In *Dawn*, the second novel, the protagonist, now known as Elisha, is eighteen years old; three years have passed since he was liberated from Buchenwald at the end of *Night*. Elisha is no longer certain of God's absolute guilt and he takes up the study of philosophy in an effort to find answers to the questions that still torment him: "Where is God to be found? In suffering or in rebellion?" He is "anxious to re-evaluate [his] revolt in an atmosphere of detachment, to view it in terms of the present" (18).[8] However, in *Dawn* he finds no answers; the trial of God is held in abeyance for the time being, while the trial of Judaism assumes a new form. Elisha joins a group of Jewish terrorists fighting the English in Palestine and is ordered by the leader of the movement to execute John Dawson, an English officer, in retaliation for the expected hanging of David ben Moshe, a member of the resistance group. Ordered to violate one of the sacred Mosaic commandments and this, as he believes, *for the sake of Jewish survival*, Elisha is caught in a tragically ironic dilemma and takes refuge in a desperate attempt to hate John Dawson: "Why do I try to hate you, John Dawson? Because my people have never known how to hate. Their tragedy . . . has stemmed from their inability to hate those who have humiliated them and from time to time exterminated them. Now our only chance lies in . . . learning . . . the art of hate. Otherwise . . . our future will only be an extension of the past . . ." (86).

Here there is reference to the code of *mentshlekhkayt*, the code that had held in check the plans of the young

8. Elie Wiesel, *Dawn* (New York, 1961).

among the newly arrived in Auschwitz to revolt against
the guards. Instead of proceeding with these plans, they
had listened to the advice of their elders: "You must never
lose faith, even when the sword hangs over your head. That
is the teaching of our sages . . ." (*Night*, 41). Perhaps
Elisha feels that a response to such a fastidious morality
was absurd then and would be now. In any case he subdues
his conscience and carries out the execution, thus acting
counter to the whole tradition of the Jewish people. Yet
the memory of the concentration camp seems to legitimize
the deed and validate the ideals of the resistance movement.
Israel was a place on the map, a cause for which men
killed and risked their lives. The justification for killing in
the cause of Israel is given by Gad, Elisha's leader, who
freely admits that shedding blood is cruel and inhuman.
There is no other choice, he avers, at this point in history:
"For generations we've wanted to be better, more pure in
heart than those who persecuted us . . . ; heretofore we've
chosen to be victims rather than executioners. . . . But
that's all over; we must be like everybody else. Murder will
not be our profession but our duty" (*Dawn*, 29–30). Here
we may observe the interesting phenomenon of Zionism
brought to trial by the code of *mentshlekhkayt*. The members of the movement, unlike the Nazis, are not simply free
to kill, even in their own self-interest. On the contrary, they
are constrained to justify their acts in the light of Jewish
Law and morality. The decision to kill can be carried out
only by denying this code. Hence, where *Night* witnessed
the loss of the religious Jew, *Dawn* describes the loss of the
moral Jew and carries the trial of Judaism a step further.

In *The Accident* the hero, a survivor of the concentration camps and a veteran of the Hebrew resistance movement, has become a newswriter for an Israeli newspaper

and now lives in New York City. Haunted by his past, guilty for having survived, believing himself "a messenger of death," he is struck down by a taxicab in Times Square, in an "accident" which can better be interpreted as an act of attempted suicide. Eliezer/Elisha has by now completely lost his will to be alive and has been overcome by a feeling of futility. This fact has not escaped Paul Russel, the young physician who first saves his life and later demands to know why he does not care about living: "During the operation. You never helped me. Not once. You abandoned me. I had to wage the fight alone. . . . You were on the other side, on the side of the enemy" (69).[9] That Dr. Russel cares profoundly about life in general, and the saving of his life in particular, is a revelation to the narrator, who, since his days in the concentration camp, has become accustomed to thinking that all men are divided into three groups: the victims, the executioners, and the passive spectators at the execution. The physician stands outside this bitter division, a man for whom saving life has become a passion: "Each prey torn away from death made him as happy as if he had won a universal victory. A defeat left dark rings under his eyes" (66). Dr. Russel's dedication to life is the first ray of hope in *The Accident*, and perhaps the first unambiguously hopeful indication in the first three novels. (Elisha's involvement with the movement in *Dawn* lends hope to his existence, at least insofar as it gives him a goal toward which to work. However, this sense of hope is diminished by the necessity for Elisha to take life.) The existence of dedicated men, exemplified by Dr. Russel, who are committed to life and thus to what God represents, even if not to God himself in a formally religious sense, is a revelation with which the narrator must

9. Elie Wiesel, *The Accident* (New York, 1962).

cope and which he must somehow fit into his mode of thought.

This revelation, by itself, would be sufficient reason to conclude that *The Accident* represents a significant turning point in the trial of Judaism within the scheme of the five novels. There is, however, yet another compelling reason: with the attempt at suicide the protagonist has made the final rejection of life and, with it, of Judaism. For in Judaism reverence for life is basic; when all else is gone the desire for self-preservation at least should remain. This is demanded by Jewish Law, supported by Jewish tradition, operative through the code of *mentshlekhkayt*. Thus the attempted suicide and the continued wish to die try Judaism even more sorely than the protestations of God's guilt which are to be found everywhere in *Night*. It follows that the renewed interest in life, brought about by the physician and Gyula, the painter, is of great significance. It begins the evolution of hope which ultimately leads to Gregor's confrontation with the Hasidic rebbe and tentative gropings toward renewed acceptance of Judaism (in the form of Hasidic Judaism) in *The Gates of the Forest*.

In *The Accident* Gyula is a spokesman for the ideals of Hasidism, presented, however, without any reference to God. This, of course, reflects the preoccupation with Jewish mysticism evident in all Wiesel's works starting with the first page of *Night*, when Eliezer asks his father to find a master to guide him in studies of the Cabala. This interest is maintained in *Night* through the character of Akiba Drumer, who was still lost in his cabalistic dreams, even in the concentration camp. More striking is Elisha's reaction to the sudden appearance in *Dawn* of Gad, who has come to enlist him in the resistance movement. Elisha responds to the visitor's simple and direct self-introduction, "I am

Gad," with the feeling that here was being uttered some "cabalistic sentence which contained an answer to every question" (19). He explains this through reference to his upbringing in the Hasidic tradition, which contains "strange stories about the Meshulah, the mysterious messenger of fate to whom nothing is impossible." Elisha feels that Gad is Meshulah, and Gad as Meshulah is irresistible to Elisha. Thus it is a foregone conclusion that Elisha will join with Gad in the resistance: "He was a messenger, a man sent by fate, to whom I could refuse nothing. I must sacrifice everything to him, even hope, if he asked it" (20).

Now, in *The Accident*, Gyula too has a message for the narrator. One day he bursts into his friend's hospital room and announces his intention to do his portrait, even though the hero is still half-dead. Gyula alone has guessed that his good friend no longer cares to live, that the "accident" was really something else, and apparently feels that the portrait will provide a useful diversion: "Don't die before I've finished your portrait . . . afterwards, I don't give a darn! But not before! Understand?" (111–112). The message here is that of the Hasidic rebbe: to counterpose joy against despair, life against death, affirmation against negation. Gyula too has an obsession: "To pit himself against fate, to force it to give human meaning to its cruelty" (113).

The portrait turns out to be far more than a diversion. After several weeks of painting and conversation, on the day before the patient is to leave the hospital, Gyula presents him with the completed painting. The narrator sees in his image a vision of the past: "I was there, facing me. My whole past was there, facing me. It was a painting in which black . . . dominated. . . . My eyes were a beating red. . . . They belonged to a man who had seen God commit the most unforgivable crime: to kill without a reason" (116). He begins to speak of the dead ones he left behind, those whom he represents among the living, those with whom he feels he belongs. "You must forget them," Gyula responds. "You must chase them from your memory" (117). Gyula goes on, insisting that man's duty is to make suffering cease: "Man must keep moving, searching, weighing, holding out his hand, offering himself, inventing himself" (118). The connection of Gyula's argument with the prescriptions of Jewish mysticism is so clear that the narrator has the sudden impression of being with Kalman the cabalist rather than with the painter. However, the argument falls on deaf ears; sensing this, in a sudden moment of rage Gyula sets fire to the portrait. As a symbolic destruction of the tormented past, Gyula's gesture is perhaps effective; for the first time the protagonist can cry and, in so doing, releases a bit of the pent-up horror. The physical recovery from near death now holds out the promise of a spiritual recovery as well. Although Gyula does not speak of God or religion, his exhortation to forget the dead and concentrate upon life is a reflection of the true meaning of the *Kaddish*. His plea is similar to one Kalman might have made and the one the Hasidic rebbe in Brooklyn in fact does make in *The Gates of the Forest*. Thus the new-found hope of the protagonist is rooted in Judaism, and the trial of Judaism begins to move in favor of the defense.

Continued movement in this same direction is a prominent feature of *The Town beyond the Wall*, Wiesel's fourth novel. In this work no significant new problems are raised, no substantially new features are added to the indictment of God and Judaism. The novel is impelled rather by the mystery of man's suffering and God's indifference, the same problems exposed and developed in the first three novels. On the other hand, *The Town beyond the Wall* makes a significant contribution toward the search for possible answers, for reasons why man must go on struggling against the evil within both God and himself. It is in this sense that the fourth novel carries forward the trial of Judaism.

The categorizing of man into victims, executioners, and indifferent observers, mentioned in *The Accident*, becomes a theme of some importance in *The Town beyond the Wall*. In fact, it provides the novel's principal plot element. The protagonist, now called Michael, is a young Jew who survived the Nazi death camps. After the war he settles in Paris as a student and eventually, after a period of hunger, obtains a position as a reporter for a Paris weekly, with an assignment to write a travel diary from Tangier. In Tangier he meets Pedro, the novel's teacher-philosopher. With the help of Pedro, who is a member of an international smuggling ring, Michael is able to satisfy his greatest wish, a trip back to the town of his childhood in Hungary. Michael is, at this point, rather vague about his reasons for wanting the trip so much. It is only after he succeeds in returning to Hungary that he understands fully the real reason for his return: to confront and humiliate one of the indifferent observers, a particular man that Michael had noticed casually watching the brutal deportation of the Jews from the town, apparently unmoved by the sight, unconcerned about the fate of these victimized men, women, and children. Michael does in fact find and confront this man, but he pays dearly for the privilege; the man reports him to the police and Michael is arrested as a foreign spy. His arrest provides the framework for the novel, whose action occurs as a series of flashbacks and imaginary dialogues with Pedro during his imprisonment and torture. The torture, undertaken to force information from Michael, takes the form of "prayers" during which the prisoner is forced to remain standing for protracted periods of time.

Upon his return to the city of his childhood Michael continues to be uncertain about his motives: "What have I come here to do? To what call had I responded?" (154).[10] He visits his house, his father's store, the place where the synagogue once stood, and although these visits are important to him, he remains convinced that he has not yet made the essential move, that there is a precise purpose for which he has come back but which he has not yet accomplished. A sudden memory at the site of the old synagogue, the starting point of the deportation of the Jews in 1944, forces the real purpose violently into his consciousness. ". . . I need to understand . . . the others—the Other—those who watched us depart for the unknown . . . without emotion . . . while we became objects—living sticks of wood . . ." (159). For Michael the single man whose face he saw long ago in the window across from the synagogue has come to represent all of the "neutrals"; "the others were only reflections of him. Copies" (159).

The confrontation itself, later that day, turns out to be inconclusive. Michael accuses the man of indifference, of cowardice, of being something less than human. He feels that this man is beneath hatred, deserving only of contempt. The spectator's rebuttal is effective: "You accuse me of cowardice. And you? What were you? A few policemen—not more than ten—led you all to the slaughterhouse: why didn't you seize their arms? Can you tell me why?" (170). In this answer there are the familiar elements which were found in *Dawn*, in the line of reasoning which finally persuaded Elisha to carry out the execution of the English officer. This rebuttal is a further setback for Judaism in its trial, for, in essence, it is an attack upon the code of *mentshlekhkayt*, the moral code which effectively prevented any large-scale uprising of Jews against the Nazis.

10. Elie Wiesel, *The Town beyond the Wall* (New York, 1964).

Against his will, Michael finds himself accepting the man's defense, conceding that he was right. Thus the confrontation remains a standoff; Michael succeeds in angering the man, in making him suffer, but not in humiliating him. Still, through the encounter Michael comes closer to the answers he has been seeking: "Man is not only an executioner, not only a victim, not only a spectator: he is all three at once" (174).

Michael's confrontation with the "spectator" reveals the importance of suffering as a motif in this novel. It is indicative that it is not the man's argument but rather his suffering that persuades Michael that he is human after all. Indeed, man's search for an appropriate response to suffering and, in particular, to the holocaust is the dominant theme of the work. A related theme is that of madness, and especially the contemplation of madness as a response to suffering. Michael's constant struggle with the desire for madness as a way to alleviate pain is foreshadowed in the book's epigraph from Dostoevsky: "I have a plan: to go mad."

The preoccupation with madness is present already in the first section, which relates how two of the students of Kalman have gone mad, presumably driven insane by the mad Kalman. Michael is Kalman's third student, and yet he remains unafraid, refusing to give up Kalman as a master, challenging madness to overtake him. The theme is repeated and reinforced in the novel's second section, which is dominated by the character of Yankel, a twelve-year-old boy who was, with Michael, a prisoner in a German concentration camp; following the war, like Michael, he was settled in Paris where he attended school. After having several painful visits with Yankel, Michael learns that the boy has been struck down by a truck and is close to death.

Seven days later Yankel dies, and Michael is drawn toward madness to alleviate his suffering: "It was at that moment that I was most tempted to take the leap . . . to roll on the floor, stick out my tongue, break into song, howl like a hurt dog: safety was there within reach, and detachment, deliverance" (100).

But Michael refuses to submit to the temptation of clinical madness and, with this refusal, responds to the tenets of the code of *mentshlekhkayt*. He recognizes madness as an easy escape: "The man who chooses death is following an impulse of liberation from the self; so is the man who chooses madness" (100). Michael rejects both death and madness as valid responses to suffering, and in so doing he shows progress beyond the position of the narrator of *The Accident*, who attempted suicide and had no desire to recover. This progress is reinforced and abetted by Pedro: "The dialogue—or the duel, if you prefer—between man and his God doesn't end in nothingness. Man may not have the last word, but he has the last cry. That moment marks the birth of art" (103).

Rejection of madness is only the first step; the next one is the discovery of an alternative plan for fathoming the mystery of man's suffering. Here Pedro shows Michael the way: "To say 'I suffer, therefore I am' is to become the enemy of man. . . . You must say 'I suffer, therefore you are.' . . . To protest against a universe of unhappiness, you had to create happiness . . . it leads to another human being. And not via absurdity" (127). This is, at heart, a plea for a life governed by the code of *mentshlekhkayt*, a rejection of suffering as an end in itself, a demand that suffering be somehow employed for the greater good of mankind. There is here a striking similarity to, and an extension of, the argument of Gyula in *The Accident*, when he pleads for life, with all its torment, over death. Unlike the narrator of *The Accident*, who remained indifferent to Gyula's plea, Michael is impressed by the argument: "Of all the words Michael ever heard Pedro speak, these were later the ones that came to his aid" (127). He comes to realize, as the narrator of *The Accident* never did, that flight into madness would destroy his humanity, make of him a "spectator" and thus something less than a man.

In the book's final section, "The Last Prayer," Michael encounters Menachem, a cellmate in the Hungarian prison who, like Nelly Sachs in *Eli*, argues for the power of prayer as a counter to man's suffering. Menachem has heard the voice of God: "It asked me questions and gave me the answers. Thanks to that, I held out; I wasn't alone" (146). He advises: "Pray, Michael. It's your only chance. Pray to God to open the source of tears within you" (147). But the answer of Nelly Sachs is unacceptable to Wiesel; Michael, still refusing to give in to God, still insisting on laughter in the face of pain, rejects Menachem's advice with heavy irony; his response to Menachem's plea for prayer is the single word "Never." Menachem predicts that Michael is headed straight for perdition, upon which Michael concedes the possibility and counters: "But I prefer to go down laughing" (147).

In contrast, Michael is unable to ignore Pedro's advice to try to help others. In the book's final pages Michael feels himself slipping downward; the smallest act becomes a major effort for him in his loneliness. Then one night Michael saves the life of a catatonic prisoner who shares his cell. Since the boy is insane, a mindless, speechless vegetable, Michael dismisses his act of heroism as worthless: "I've saved a body. A body with a sleeping mind and a dead soul. I'm not proud" (182). Pedro meets Michael's

sense of futility with a plan for a positive course of action:
" 'Recreate the universe. Restore that boy's sanity. Cure
him. He'll save you. . . . The only valuable protest . . . is
one rooted in . . . humanity. Remaining human—in spite
of all temptations and humiliations—is the only way . . .
against the Other, whatever it may be' " (182–183). Here
Pedro goes to the heart of the code of *mentshlekhkayt* in
suggesting that any man, even an insane man, is worth saving, in asserting the mutual responsibility of men to each
other, and finally in recognizing that man's very salvation
is bound up with his fellow man.

Michael's response to Pedro's plan is immediate and
dramatic. He "welcomed the dawn as a new man. His
strength flowed back" (183). Of course, Michael is not
able to cure the boy, but he devotes himself completely to
the task and finally wrings a gesture, small and insignificant,
but human, from his patient. This small gesture, an ex-
tended hand, affects Michael profoundly, and, encouraged,
he continues his efforts until several days later he sees in
the boy's eyes the first glimpses of "human thirst, human
suffering, a human question." Michael is overcome with
joy, hope, strength, and now feels he is able to "push back
the night with [his] bare hands" (185). Pedro's prediction
—"Cure him. He'll save you"—has been fulfilled. Michael
has found salvation in bringing a spark of humanity back
to the life of an afflicted fellow human being. His final
position, his final answer to the mystery of man's suffering,
is summarized in his lesson to the boy. He speaks of "the
art and the necessity of clinging to humanity, never desert-
ing humanity" (187–188). Then he goes on: "To flee to a
sort of Nirvana . . . through indifference or . . . apathy
—is to oppose humanity. . . . It's harder to remain human
than to try to leap beyond humanity." Michael touches

upon his former obsession with the neutral "spectator" when he reaches the capstone of his position: "To be indifferent—for whatever reason—is to deny not only the validity of existence, but also its beauty. Betray, and you are a man; torture your neighbor, you're still a man. Evil is human; weakness is human; indifference is not" (188). Michael's profound insight reflects an important development in Wiesel's point of view, a significant change from his previous position. Here Wiesel has completely rejected the indifference toward life of the narrator of *The Accident*. Madness and suicide are dismissed as futile and are replaced by concern for man and involvement with humanity. (This change in attitude, based as it is firmly upon the code of *mentshlekhkayt*, reveals the power of the moral code.)

The novel ends upon an unalloyed note of optimism. Michael gives the boy the biblical name of Eliezer, which means "God has answered my prayer" (189). This is an indication that Michael, though rejecting Menachem's plea to trust in the efficacy of prayer, does not completely repudiate God. Indeed, he has previously confessed his inability to do so: "I want to blaspheme, and I can't quite manage it." Although he shouts, shakes his fist, screams with rage, "it's still a way of telling Him that He's there, that He exists . . ." (123).

The legend closing the novel, in which it is related how God and man exchanged places, forces upon us the conclusion that man is as guilty as God for the suffering in the world, and thus that a repudiation of God entails a repudiation of man as well. The message of the legend carries with it a call to action: since God is somewhere within man, man must struggle to free the spark of godliness within himself in order to free God. Michael has responded to this call in his effort to help the idiot boy; because he has come to the aid of man, repudiation of God is impossible.

By the end of *The Town beyond the Wall* Wiesel has moved to a neutral position on the question of the guilt of God for the crimes of the holocaust. God is neither vindicated nor wholly to blame. The following novel, *The Gates of the Forest*, presents a position on this question which is a logical outgrowth of the final one of *The Town beyond the Wall*, where Wiesel was seeking a solution without God, that is, solely within man. In *The Gates of the Forest* the attempt at separation of God from man is abandoned; Gregor, the protagonist, comes to realize that for him, at least, a solution without God is impossible, that the separation is an artificial one and cannot be sustained. Here Wiesel is responding not only to the code of *mentschlekh-kayt* but as well to the traditional role of God in Judaism, according to which the ultimate goal of service to man is service to God, and conversely. This, finally, is the true meaning of *mentshlekhkayt* in its fullest sense. Recognizing the ultimate interdependence of God and man, Wiesel finds within traditional Judaism an acceptable solution to the mystery of man's suffering. With this solution he vindicates Judaism.

Gregor arrives at his final philosophical position, his vindication of Judaism, primarily as a response to discussions with Gavriel, the teacher-philosopher of the novel. Gavriel, carrying on the tradition of Gad in *Dawn*, Gyula in *The Accident*, and especially Pedro in *The Town beyond the Wall*, conveys a sense of mystery, cares intensely about life and man's place in it, and, through philosophical-religious discussion, exerts a powerful influence over Gregor's thought. In a real sense the philosopher-teachers in all of Wiesel's novels are extensions of Moche the beadle of *Night* and

Kalman the cabalist of *The Town beyond the Wall*, through whom Wiesel makes known to us the importance to him of his childhood teachers. In the later novels the importance of the philosopher-teacher has grown, so that Pedro plays a far more influential role in Michael's life than does Gad in Elisha's or Gyula in the life of the nameless narrator of *The Accident*. In *The Gates of the Forest* Gavriel assumes a significance at least equal to that of Pedro, reappearing at a critical juncture in each of the four sections into which the novel is divided, but each time in a new guise, playing a new role.

In "Spring," the first section of the novel, we once again encounter the Jewish youth, now called Gregor, in Hungary during World War II. The setting is a mountain cave outside the boy's village, which has been proclaimed *Judenrein* by the Nazis; Gregor, leaving his family behind, has managed to escape deportation by hiding in the cave. He is visited there by a stranger who speaks mysteriously about having lost his name: "It went away one day, without reason, without excuse. It forgot to take me along. That's why I have no name" (*Gates*, 19). Ascertaining that the stranger is a Jew, Gregor admits that he himself is a Jew hiding from the Germans. The stranger protests that Gregor is not a Jewish name and persuades Gregor to reveal his original name, Gavriel. The exposure of his true name inspires Gregor to make a gift of the name to the nameless stranger. This stranger, now called Gavriel, is the philosopher-teacher of "Spring."

There is speculation by both Gregor and Gavriel about the meaning of their encounter: "If our paths have crossed, it must be that our meeting conceals some meaning" (29). Whatever the meaning, Gavriel is determined that there is to be one: "If . . . our meeting seems to have no significance, then we must impose one upon it" (29). At least part of the meaning seems to be the message Gavriel has brought to deliver to Gregor. This message, reminiscent of those of Gyula and Pedro, is a call to respond to the code of *mentshlekhkayt*, to assert life over death, to work for the good of man, to continue to hope rather than give up in despair. Almost the first words Gavriel utters to Gregor contain the germ of this message: "I want you to value your life. I demand that to win this war, I want you strong and victorious" (29). Even Gavriel's interpretation of the loss of his name becomes part of this hopeful thesis. He asserts that during a war there is a separation between a man and his name, that it is possible for a name to have its own fate, "independent of the life and fate of its bearer" (19). The crux of his argument comes with the claim that although the Germans kill the Jews, they are not able to kill their names. "The Talmud teaches us that deliverance will come because Israel has not changed its name" (25). The message here is that although individual Jews may be killed, even by the millions, the Jewish people will survive as long as God, the everlasting, does. By separating themselves from their names, Jews can make it possible for the Jewish presence in the world to survive their own deaths. This is the essential meaning of Gavriel's loss of name that Gregor at first found so puzzling.

Gavriel's message of hope is an extension of Gregor's dream of the previous night in which his dead grandfather spoke to him: "You're letting yourself go. . . . You must fight against sadness; it weakens you and paves the way for death. You'll be lost unless you overcome it" (21). The grandfather, who had been a Hasid, a follower of the rebbe of Wizanitz, has in fact delivered the message of Hasidic Judaism, a message to be repeated in the novel's fourth section by the Hasidic rebbe in Brooklyn. It is a plea for reliance on the power of faith and ecstasy, for pitting joy and laughter against suffering in order to drive suffering out. In this connection it is significant that Gregor's first meeting with Gavriel begins with Gavriel's laughter; first Gavriel laughs and he speaks only afterward to explain to Gregor: "I'm listening to the war and I'm laughing" (17).

In "Spring" the trial of Judaism remains at essentially the same level of development as it had reached at the end of *The Town beyond the Wall*. Like Michael in that novel, Gregor is unable to respond to the power of faith and prayer: "Men love and kill one another; God bids them pray and yet their prayers change nothing" (19). Instead, Gregor believes that God can and must be challenged when he has wronged man. This, in fact, is the meaning of the story of Shlomo, whose father was a judge in the rabbinic court, and who rebelled against Jewish Law and tradition by appearing in front of the synagogue on Sabbath morning smoking a cigarette. Shlomo's father responded by considering him lost, no longer his son. In discussing the incident with his son, Gregor's father imparted the lesson that the man who makes a free choice, particularly against centuries of tradition, is accomplishing his destiny and thus deserves special respect. The striking aspect of this is the assertion of man's right, and under appropriate circumstances perhaps *responsibility*, to rebel against God and free himself from him.

This same theme is enlarged upon in Gavriel's story of Moshe the beadle. Convinced that Moshe was the Messiah come to earth, Gavriel entreated him to take action and to precipitate events, to stop the massacre of the Jewish people that had already begun in the cities of Europe. Gavriel pointed to passages in the Talmud and the Midrash, in order to demonstrate that it was Moshe's duty to disobey God in order to save the Jews from complete destruction. However, Moshe, feeling helpless and panic-stricken, failed to respond. Gavriel could not accept this impotence: "If this is God's will, then deny it! . . . impose your will upon His . . ." (57). At the end Moshe did nothing and was eventually himself swept away by the holocaust. This episode is significant not only because it expresses Gavriel's belief that man must, on occasion, rise up against God but also because it puts Judaism on trial in yet another way. Gavriel concludes that since the Messiah came and accomplished nothing, it is hopeless to continue to wait for his coming, as Jews are expected to do: the Messiah came and nothing changed. "The Messiah came and the world is a vast slaughterhouse, as it was before" (56).

Gavriel's trial of Judaism, his appeal to action against God, is quite unlike Eliezer's bitter repudiation of God in *Night*. Like Michael in *The Town beyond the Wall*, Gavriel is unable to reject God completely: "God's final victory . . . lies in man's inability to reject Him. You think you're cursing Him, but your curse is praise" (42). Here, once more, the important idea of the legend at the end of *The Town beyond the Wall* is introduced: that God shares man's fate, that he is not wholly to blame for the world's evil, that perhaps he has not the power, alone, to stop the world's sufferings but can only do so with man's help. Thus God would appear to be vindicated here of much of the guilt of which he was accused in *Night*.

Although God is on trial in Gavriel's call to action against him, Judaism is not; indeed, Gavriel's appeal to Moshe to take action against God is justified on the basis of sacred Jewish writings, the Talmud and the Midrash. Ultimately, at the point when Gavriel asserts the value of human life as the highest authority, the justification involves the Jewish code of *mentshlekhkayt* as well: "No good deed equals in meaning and importance that of saving a human life. If there is a question of bringing help to the dying, even the laws of the Sabbath may be broken" (55). In a real sense Gavriel is here calling upon Moshe to rise against God for the sake of remaining within God. He argues that preservation of life is God's highest priority, as it is man's, and thus takes precedence even over the sacred Sabbath observation. This is only one of several indications in "Spring" of the overriding importance of the code of *mentshlekhkayt*.

Another indication is evident in Gregor's reaction to Gavriel's story of Joseph de-la-Reina, the medieval cabalist who overcame Satan and threw him into chains, only to release him because of pity for Satan's tears. This release had the unfortunate effect of forcing the Messiah, already on the verge of arrival, to return to his prison indefinitely. Gregor astonishes Gavriel by asserting that the rabbi was right. "I don't want salvation to come through fire, through cruelty, and through the sacrifice of others" (28). The attitude reflected here grows out of that tenet of the code which forbids advancement at the expense of another human being, even if he is evil. In his interpretation of the ending of Gavriel's story, Gregor extends this tenet to forbid cruelty even to the evil (here symbolized by Satan) and even if this cruelty achieves salvation and the coming of the Messiah.

The code of *mentshlekhkayt* not only provides justification for Gavriel's call to action against God but, additionally, supplies the feeling of subdued hopefulness which gradually emerges in "Spring." Rather early in this section of the novel, Gregor expresses his despair in a reference to the sun, which warms only "out of habit or out of bore-

dom. People don't interest it any longer" (18). At the end
of "Spring" the sun is mentioned again, but this time as
a sign of hope: "The sun gives life and sustains it, all will
be well" (58). Gavriel has by this time imparted to Gregor
his message of action based upon reverence for humanity
and laughter in the face of death. The section closes with
Gavriel's sacrifice of his own life in order to save Gregor
from death. In this heroic act Gavriel justifies his teachings,
proving that man is capable of acting in accordance with
the code of *mentshlekhkayt*. When captured by the soldiers and their dogs, Gavriel bursts suddenly into overwhelming laughter, thus carrying out to the last his message
of defiance of death by laughter.

In "Summer," the novel's second section, Gregor escapes
from his cave and finds shelter in the house of Maria, who
formerly was employed as a servant by Gregor's family.
Maria decides to disguise Gregor as her deaf-mute nephew,
the son of her libertine sister Ileana. This decision to protect Gregor at great risk to herself continues the theme
of heroism begun with Gavriel's sacrifice: "The old servant
had decided to struggle . . . against the monstrous ma-
chine of war" (71). The hope for mankind, it seems, is at
least partially founded upon individual acts of heroism performed by people as individuals.

Gregor in his turn is involved in an act of heroism precipitated by his selection to play a deaf-mute Judas in the
school play. Under instructions from the Ministry of Education to deal with "the hatred of the Jews and its justification," Constantine Stefan, the schoolteacher, is inspired
to dramatize the story of the traitor Judas (96). By default,
since none of the schoolchildren is willing to portray the
hated Jew, Gregor is chosen to play the part. During the
performance the other actors are supposed to go through

the motions of beating Judas; instead, they are moved to inflict a genuine beating upon Gregor, and in this they receive the support of the audience. For a time Gregor silently withstands their abuse and blows, until he is bleeding freely from the head and seems in danger of his life. Then (as the villagers think) miraculously, Gregor speaks out firmly: "Men and women of this village, listen to me!" (113). There follows a confrontation between persecuted Judaism and the usual Christian dogma on the question of Judas's betrayal of Jesus, as Gregor undertakes to humiliate the terror-stricken villagers, who are convinced that they are witnesses to a miracle. In his moment of heroic triumph, Gregor achieves a position of power over the Jew-hating villagers and flirts with the possibility of exposing openly the damaging secrets he had heard from the villagers themselves when they believed him to be a deaf-mute. If he did this, they would hate one another openly instead of hating the Jews. But once again the code of *mentshlekhkayt* exerts an influence, the Jewish inability to exact vengeance manifests itself. Instead of betraying the villagers, Gregor exposes himself to danger by revealing his own true identity. In so doing, Gregor has taken on the heroic proportions of Gavriel, challenging death and apparently not fearing it, feeling at one with his fellow Jews who were dying at the same moment: "Gregor did not flinch. At this same moment . . . ten thousand Jews were tumbling into ditches. He would not die alone" (119). In this moment Gregor has fulfilled his promise to Gavriel; he has remembered Gavriel's companions who died heroically, with "a pride that came down . . . from an earlier age [preventing] them from bowing down even before God" (30). This pride is rooted in the Jewish covenant with God, which asserts man's moral equality with God and which is contrary to Christian doctrine.

In addition to the Judas episode, "Summer" presents
another confrontation between Judaism and Christianity,
this one bearing on the trial of God and emphasizing the
sharply differing attitudes toward God in the two religious
traditions. This confrontation involves the village priest,
who, having sheltered a fugitive Jew to save him from the
Nazis, undertakes at the same time to save his soul, to
bring him to the light. The priest suggests that the Jew
should be thankful to God for saving his life and because
the trials of the Jews were nearing an end. But the Jew
refuses to thank God in time of war. He owes God nothing. Christian doctrine, as understood by the village priest
at any rate, does not admit the possibility that God might
be evil or in error, and the reaction of the priest is the expected one. Shocked by the Jew's rebellious words, the
priest sends him from his house and to his death. The contrast between this episode and the Judas episode is striking:
the priest acts upon religious principle but, in so doing,
violates human life. As Judas, Gregor too acted upon principle, but the principle was that of the code of *mentshlekhkayt*, which prevented him from harming the villagers when
he had it within his power to do so. The same principle of
mentshlekhkayt operates to protect the priest who had
temporarily sheltered the Jew from the Germans. For when
the Germans capture the Jew, he does not expose the
priest, even under torture. The point is that while Judaism
shares with Christianity the principle of reverence for God,
it gives even higher priority to the principle of reverence
for life. This divergence of principle explains why it is
possible for Judaism to condone, sometimes even encourage,
accusations against God, whereas Christianity cannot.

It is reasonable to suppose that in agreeing to play the
part of Judas, Gregor was hoping for the opportunity to
somehow utilize the stage to expose the traditional Chris-

tian view of the Judas-Jesus relationship as a fraud. In carrying out this plan, he brings himself in great danger, from which he is rescued only at the last possible moment by the mysterious Count Petruskanu, the mayor of the village, who takes Gregor to the Jewish partisans hiding in the nearby forest. We are led to conjecture that Petruskanu is in reality Gavriel returned in a new guise. For Gregor and Petruskanu communicated silently while the count was seated in the audience and the young Jew was undergoing the beating onstage, and thus the impression is left that Petruskanu and Gregor have met before, that the count is somehow connected with Gavriel; both are mysterious, both are heroic, both are on the side of justice. The silent communication continues after Gregor has been led to safety. At this point Gregor senses that Petruskanu is destined to have the same significance in his life as did Gavriel; furthermore, Gavriel, in new guises, will continue to appear at critical junctures in Gregor's life in the future. Gregor's intuition proves to be well-founded, for he is to encounter Leib in "Autumn," the novel's third section, and a stranger whom he takes for Gavriel in "Winter," the final section.

Leib, Gregor's childhood friend, is the leader of the partisan group to which Petruskanu takes Gregor after the rescue. With his arrival among the partisans, Gregor informs a disbelieving Leib of the Nazi program for the methodical annihilation of the Jewish people, about the deportations and extermination camps. Gregor tells Leib about Gavriel, from whom the information had first come, and Leib decides that the partisans should try to free Gavriel because he seems to have information that the partisans do not. Leib's plan for freeing Gavriel from prison involves himself, Gregor, and Clara, Leib's loved one, who spend several days in the town in constant danger, trying to ascertain whether Gavriel is alive and, if so, where he is being held. Unfortunately the scheme backfires: Gavriel is not found and Leib is taken prisoner. Leib's capture (and certain death) poses a new problem for Gregor—that of shame.

Gregor's shame at his own survival after Leib's death is reinforced by the accusations of the partisan group when he returns to the forest. There is a quasi trial during which Zeide, the new partisan leader, hints strongly that Gregor is somehow to blame for the failure of the plan and for Leib's death. In a sense, the Judas episode is echoed in this scene, for, like the villagers during the school play, the partisans here try to fix blame upon a single man for a failure in which they all share responsibility. Just as the Jews, particularly Judas, are made to bear the blame for the Crucifixion, so is Gregor held responsible for the tragic reversal of a scheme upon which all the partisans had agreed. The search for a scapegoat is not restricted to Gentiles; the Jewish partisans too are capable of acting contrary to the code of *mentshlekhkayt*, according to which they should have accepted their share of the responsibility for Leib's death.

But even now the code of *mentshlekhkayt* triumphs once more, for Gregor has a sudden realization of his own share of the responsibility as well as that of the other partisans: "The injustice perpetrated in an unknown land concerns me; I am responsible. He who is not among the victims is with the executioners. . . . [The holocaust] implicated not only Abraham or his son, but their God as well" (168). Again the code of *mentshlekhkayt* has brought God to trial, has implicated him in the world's injustice, but in contrast to *Night*, it is recognized that man shares the responsibility with God. Furthermore, just as man shares guilt with God, so does God share suffering with man. The partisan Yehuda lectures Gregor on this point: "The Talmud tells us that God suffers with man . . . in order to strengthen the bonds between creation and the creator. God chooses to suffer in order to better understand man" (180). The answer to man's suffering does not lie in hatred, for, as Yehuda points out, to hate the executioner is to play his game and to accept an exchange on his terms. Rather, the solution is to be found in man's love for his fellows.

The novel's closing section, "Winter," finds Gregor living in New York after the war. For some reason unknown to him, Gregor is drawn toward a Hasidic synagogue. Among the Hasids he begins to dwell once again on God's injustice to man, and the trial of Judaism begins anew. In his first meeting with the Hasidic rebbe, Gregor presents Auschwitz as evidence against God. The rebbe's response indicts man as both executioner and victim but does not attempt to vindicate God. The dialogue is continued at a later meeting during which Gregor insists that God bears his share of the responsibility for man's fall. It is important that, unlike Eliezer in *Night*, Gregor is here asserting only that God *shares* in the guilt, not that he bears it alone, and thus there is an implicit, unspoken, recognition that man too shares in this guilt. It is interesting that Gregor and the rebbe agree upon the basic notion that God and man together share the blame for the world's injustice, for the holocaust. Their disagreement is one of emphasis, Gregor stressing God's culpability, the rebbe, man's.

There is a disagreement as well concerning man's proper response to the holocaust. Gregor feels that man should defy God, cry out against him. At the same time, he feels, man should strive to act toward his fellow man in accordance with the code of *mentshlekhkayt*. The rebbe agrees that this response is a worthy one, that indeed man's sal-

vation is dependent partly on his immersion in the code of
mentshlekhkayt. But instead of defiance of God, the rebbe
advocates the Hasidic way of song, dance, prayer, and joy:
"Who says that power comes from a shout, an outcry
rather than from a prayer? . . . The man who goes singing
to his death is the brother of the man who goes to death
fighting" (196). The rebbe does concede that God is guilty,
that he has become the ally of evil, of death, and of murder. But he is not content to stop with the accusation
against God; he insists upon a constructive response from
man.

This, finally, is the irreducible core of the dilemma. The
recognition of God's guilt is, in itself, no solution to the
problem of evil in the world, not a viable response to the
holocaust. In spite of everything, man is fated to go on,
and he must continually make an effort to infuse meaning
into life. The new insight Gregor has gained in his discussions with the rebbe comes to light in his later conversation
with the mysterious stranger in the Hasidic synagogue, the
one whom Gregor takes to be and addresses as Gavriel.
Gregor repeatedly implores the stranger to speak, to impart
his wisdom as he had done long ago in the cave in Transyl-
vania. However, the stranger's response is minimal, limited,
in fact, to questions designed to draw Gregor out, to make
him reveal his past. Gradually, as Gregor does tell of his
past life, of his relationship with Clara, it becomes irrelevant whether the stranger is in fact Gavriel. For we become
aware that Gregor no longer is in need of Gavriel's message,
that he has by now internalized it and made it an integral
part of himself. Indeed, Gregor has a message of his own
for the stranger: "Nothing is easier than to live in a clois-
tered universe where I am alone with God alone, against
God. . . . The man who chooses solitude and its riches
is on the side of those who are against man; [the future is

not virgin;] it is mortgaged from the first day, from the first cry" (219).

Clearly Gregor is now prepared to act in accordance with the rebbe's teachings, to adopt the Hasidic way; he is ready to seek constructive alternatives to hopelessness. Thus it is natural and fitting that Gregor once again adopts his Jewish name, Gavriel, and joins the *Minyan* in the synagogue for morning service. Gregor is prepared now to live without the Gavriel of the cave, for, in a sense, he has himself become that Gavriel. The reappearance of Gavriel as the mysterious, uncommunicative stranger among the Hasids has crystallized this development in Gregor, who, until this point, has been unaware of his own strength. He finally realizes that he no longer needs to seek Gavriel and the wisdom Gavriel has to bestow. During the service Gregor prays with a fervor that he has not attained since his childhood days, before the holocaust destroyed his world. He resolves to take up once again the struggle to make life worth living and to remain with Clara, although he no longer loves her. For he concludes that one cannot chase mirages. "It's up to us to see to it that the earth itself is not a mirage" (223). Thus the novel ends with the sense that man's tragedy not only can but *must* be leavened with a determination to survive and a modicum of hope.

In Hasidic Judaism Gregor has found an approach toward the possibility of rebuilding a meaningful, viable mode of life. Thus in the end Judaism, through Hasidism and the code of *mentshlekhkayt*, is vindicated in its trial, while the trial of God remains essentially unresolved, Man and God sharing in the suffering of the world, the guilt for the existence of evil, and the hope for the future of mankind.

FIVE

Jewish America: Bernard Malamud

The *shtetl* world, whose life and death is chron-
icled by Singer and Wiesel, is separated from the world of
the Jewish-American novelists by distance, time, and vast
cultural differences. Nevertheless, the interplay of the two
principal themes, the trial of Judaism and the code of
mentshlekhkayt, provides an essential link which is common to Singer and Wiesel on the one hand and Roth,
Malamud, and Bellow on the other. While Malamud and
Bellow in particular have been greatly moved by the events
of the holocaust, a circumstance which establishes a possible
further link to Wiesel, they and Roth as well are preoccupied with man's moral evolution, a theme of great importance in Wiesel's novels and in Singer's *Magician of Lublin*.
J. C. Landis has commented upon this aspect of Malamud's
fiction, connecting it with the code of *mentshlekhkayt*:
"What was implicit in Malamud's first novel . . . became
explicit in *The Assistant* and in the novels that followed it
. . . —the evolution of man into mentsh, the slow, painful
discovery of the ways of mentshlekhkayt." [1] Though Landis
says nothing of Roth, he and Malamud in fact converge in
their overall moral outlook. For both of them "seem involved in a similar effort to feel and think with their Jew-

1. J. C. Landis, "Reflections on American Jewish Writers," *Jewish Book Annual*, XXV (1967–68), 146.

ishness . . . and usually it is back to the heart that their work leads us: to its suffering and its trials and, particularly, to its deep moral potency." [2]

Indeed, evolution into *mentsh* is a major element in Roth's story "Eli, the Fanatic." [3] A lawyer in the middle-class Jewish community of suburban Woodenton, New York, Eli Peck undergoes a moral development, emerging as "the only member of the community seriously concerned with saving the human image." [4]

A Jewish survivor of the European holocaust, Leo Tzuref has purchased a sagging mansion at the edge of town and converted it to a home and Yeshiva for eighteen orphaned Jewish children, survivors of Nazi concentration camps. The reaction of the new suburbanites, one of hysteria in the face of the "Goddam fanatics," is rationalized in a letter to Tzuref from Eli Peck, who has been engaged by Woodenton's Jews to take the necessary legal action to force the Yeshiva's removal. Eli's letter, which reveals a sensitivity to the true nature of the problem the Yeshiva's presence has visited upon his fellow Jews—embarrassment and fear of becoming identified with the newcomers in the eyes of the Protestant community—proposes a compromise. The Jews of Woodenton will forgo legal action proposed against the Yeshiva "for failure to comply with township zoning ordinances," provided only that the Yeshiva's activities remain confined to the Yeshiva grounds and (in a condition aimed directly at Tzuref's assistant, the man in the black outfit) that Yeshiva personnel appear "in the streets and stores of

2. Theodore Solotaroff, "Philip Roth and the Jewish Moralists," *Chicago Review*, XIII (Winter, 1959), 90.

3. Philip Roth, "Eli, the Fanatic," in *Goodbye Columbus* (New York, 1969).

4. Harold Fisch, "The Hero as Jew: Reflections on Herzog," *Judaism*, XVII (Winter, 1968), 46.

Woodenton" only if "they are attired in clothing usually associated with American life in the 20th century" (189).

Eli's attempt at compromise, contrary to the explicit instructions given him by the spokesmen for Woodenton's Jewish community, who insist upon the Yeshiva's removal, is only the first indication that his sympathies are divided, that he is far less than enthusiastic about the assignment he has been given. As the story develops, in fact, we are made increasingly aware that Eli, in contrast to his fellow Jews of Woodenton, is a *mentsh*, whose instincts rebel against causing Tzuref and his flock any further suffering. He is revolted at the prospect of forcing the newcomers out to find a new home elsewhere, as he feels deeply responsible for his fellow man. His sense of responsibility extends not only to the poor Jews of the Yeshiva but to the comfortable, somewhat smug, and insular middle-class Jewish community of Woodenton as well. This dual responsibility complicates his attempts to deal with Tzuref in the question of the Yeshiva's alleged zoning-law violation. At one point in Eli's second conversation with Tzuref, for example, the head of the Yeshiva argues that he and his children have suffered inordinately already and are therefore entitled to expect the Jews of Woodenton to leave them in peace: " 'They won't,' Eli said. 'But you, Mr. Peck, how about you?' 'I am them, they are me, Mr. Tzuref.' 'Ach! You are us, we are you!' " (192). In this interchange Eli has attempted to carry out his obligation to those he represents by identifying himself completely with them. However, Tzuref obviously has sensed that the lawyer's real sympathies lie elsewhere, and he proceeds to play on them: " 'What you call law, I call shame. The heart, Mr. Peck, the heart is law! God!' . . . 'They hide their shame. And you, Mr. Peck, you are shameless?' " (192).

This conversation with Tzuref strengthens Eli's sense of personal obligation toward the Yeshiva and he decides, over his wife's objections, to contribute his own clothes to Mr. Tzuref's assistant, so that this "greenie" can shed the inflammatory black outfit and appear less conspicuous during his periodic visits to Woodenton. On the way to the Yeshiva with the clothing Eli attempts to find justification for the attitude of Woodenton's middle-class Jews toward the Eastern European newcomers. "Maybe there just had to be this communal toughness—or numbness—to protect [the] blessing [of peace and safety] . . . to live takes guts" (202). His line of reasoning, reminiscent of Gad's justification of the execution of John Dawson, the English officer in Wiesel's *Dawn*, amounts to a rationale for the Jews to abandon their traditional sense of communal responsibility and to adopt a purely pragmatic stance vis-à-vis the world at large. Like Elisha in *Dawn*, Eli Peck is drawn only momentarily to this point of view, as becomes clear during the events of the next day, the climactic day of the story and of Eli's life, when the true strength of his devotion to the code of *mentshlekhkayt* becomes evident.

Early in the morning Tzuref's assistant appears in Woodenton dressed in Eli's J. Press suit instead of the usual black garb, and, as Solotaroff has pointed out, "everyone is delighted and satisfied—except Peck, for by now he has become involved in deeper issues within himself. Moved, despite his reason, by Tzuref's appeal to the heart instead of the law . . . by the suffering that the Yeshiva people represent . . . and by Tzuref's question of which of the two communities Peck really belongs to, the lawyer has become vaguely aware that his best suit is not enough." [5] Eli's distress is deepened by the first of his two confrontations with the assistant when, in his tour of Woodenton, the latter

5. Solotaroff, p. 92.

walks by the lawyer's house: "He stopped and put a hand to his hat. . . . The fingers fiddled, fumbled . . . they traveled down the fellow's face. . . . They dabbed the eyes, ran the length of the nose. . . . To Eli the fingers said, *I have a face, I have a face at least. . . . The face is all right, I can keep it?*" (204–205). This is followed immediately by the climactic moment when Eli discovers the assistant's Hasidic clothing at his back door. For reasons not clear even to himself, he removes his own clothes, dresses in the black outfit, and walks to the Yeshiva to confront Tzuref's assistant once again.

This second confrontation reveals an Eli Peck who has gone far beyond revulsion at the thought of forcing the Yeshiva from Woodenton, beyond his earlier feeling that compelling the assistant to give up his clothes was itself an unjust and immoral act. For, far from identifying himself with Woodenton's Jews, Eli now identifies strongly with the Hasidic assistant. After Eli makes a futile attempt to communicate with him, the assistant points several times in the direction of Woodenton, and Eli slowly comes to realize that he is being asked to return to town to show himself there in the black suit. Eli is unable to resist an apparent need to do as the assistant has directed; greeting his friends with the Hebrew salutation "Shalom," he walks deliberately through the heart of Woodenton's shopping district, with predictable results: "Everybody . . . was aware that Eli Peck . . . was having a breakdown. Everybody except Eli Peck. He knew what he did was not insane . . ." (212).

As Dan Isaac points out, the question of Eli's sanity is an important one, bearing, as it does, directly on the "validity and courage" of his act.[6] Isaac goes on to make a convincing case that Eli is indeed sane and describes the *modus*

6. Dan Isaac, "In Defense of Philip Roth," *Chicago Review*, XVII (Fall, 1964), 91.

operandi of the trial of Judaism in this story: "Eli is to be taken very seriously, because within him two competing cultures are struggling for dominance. America's home-made moral system of rational pragmatism does battle with a weaker but more ancient and durable adversary, traditional Judaism." [7] The clue we are given to Eli's soundness of mind is his own realization "that he'd *chosen* to be crazy," and "if you chose to be crazy, then you weren't crazy" (213). This is, on the contrary, one of the truly sane moments of Eli's life, for "as his neighbors uttered each syllable of his name, he felt each syllable shaking all his bones. He knew who he was down to his marrow—they were telling him" (212).

He crowns his act by proceeding to the hospital where he sees his newly born son, resolves to continue wearing the black suit, and makes a resolution concerning his child as well: "He'd make the kid wear it. . . . Cut it down when the time came. A smelly hand-me-down, whether the kid liked it or not!" (215). Here Eli is serving notice that he intends his conversion to remain an enduring fact of his life, that it is to be a part of his son's inheritance. This final hospital scene ends with two interns drugging Eli in order to calm him: "The drug calmed his soul, but did not touch it where the blackness had reached" (216). "What we have here," Isaac points out, "is medical science, metaphoric for all of modern thought, winning a false and superficial victory over ancient Judaism. A false victory because the black . . . represents the strange power of an authentic religion that touches an area of the soul inaccessible to tranquilizing drugs." [8]

Judaism, then, is victorious in its trial. With his single compulsive yet courageous act, through his adherence to

7. *Ibid.*, p. 93.
8. *Ibid.*, p. 94.

human values, and by steadfastly remaining a *mentsh,* Eli has vindicated Judaism, raising it from the lowly estate to which it has been brought by the Jewish community. That Eli understands the consequences of his act clearly at the beginning of his walk through Woodenton is a measure of the new-found strength of his attachment to the moral code. Thus in the final analysis what Roth rejects is not Judaism but Jewish life in America, "not because it is too Jewish, but because it is not Jewish enough, because it is so dominated by and infused with the American ethos that it partakes of the same corruption, offering no significant alternative." [9] In my view Roth *has* shown that Judaism offers a significant alternative, the difficult one chosen by Eli Peck.

If Roth stresses the corruption of traditional Jewish values among modern American middle-class Jews, the works of Bernard Malamud, as a general rule, tend to emphasize the persistence of these values uncorrupted and the relevance of the Jewish tradition of idealism to life in present-day America.

The importance to a writer of the code of *mentshlekh-kayt,* of the sense of communal responsibility, has been strongly emphasized by Malamud himself: "The purpose of the writer . . . is to keep civilization from destroying itself." [10] That Malamud's literary production is consistent with his professed "writer's code" becomes evident upon examination of *The Assistant,* which can be read as a kind of *Bildungsroman* chronicling the development of Frank Alpine and his ultimate conversion to

9. Marie Syrkin, "The Fun of Self-Abuse," *Midstream,* XV (Apr., 1969), 64.

10. Joseph Wershba, "Not Horror but 'Sadness,'" *New York Post* (Sunday, Sept. 14, 1958), M2. Interview.

Judaism. The fictional framework within which Malamud carries out Alpine's conversion is the classical one of master and apprentice, prophet and disciple, and eventually, perhaps, father and son. For Alpine's transformation is effected by his imitation and gradual adoption of the mannerisms and speech, thought patterns, and, ultimately, way of life and religion of Morris Bober, the Jewish storekeeper who serves as Frank's model of the moral life, the life lived in accordance with the code of *mentshlekhkayt*. Indeed, Morris functions in *The Assistant* in much the same way as do Wiesel's philosopher-teachers, Gyula in *The Accident*, Pedro in *The Town beyond the Wall*, and Gavriel in *The Gates of the Forest*.

Despite important differences of age, cultural background, and moral outlook, there are similarities between Frank and Morris evident almost from the outset of the novel, for both, in their propensity to hard luck, strongly resemble the classical Jewish *shlemiel*. Morris's history is one of loss. Buying the grocery store, he lost an opportunity for the education he had always wanted; later he lost his small son, Ephraim; now he is in danger of going bankrupt and losing the store, his half-hearted attempts to sell it having met with failure. In a complaint that is strikingly reminiscent of the personal epigrams of the twelfth-century Hebrew-Spanish poet Ibn Ezra, Morris establishes his credentials as a genuine *shlemiel*: "When the store was good, who wanted to sell? After came bad times, who wanted to buy?" (18).[11] It is thus consistent with Bober's history that matters are made even worse when, after a long day in the store during which the grocer takes in barely ten dollars, he is robbed and beaten with a gun: "He fell without a cry. The end fitted the day. It was his luck, others had better" (25).

11. Bernard Malamud, *The Assistant* (New York, 1957).

Alpine, too, at the age of twenty-five, already seems destined for a life of hard luck. Feeling guilty for his part in the robbery, Frank returns to help Morris and tells the grocer about his life: "With me one wrong thing leads to another and it ends in a trap. I want the moon so all I get is cheese" (31–32). Morris is struck by the young man's resemblance to himself: "I am sixty and he talks like me" (33). With this, the first conversation between the two, Frank's apprenticeship to Morris has begun. Although Frank has taken part in the robbery, there are rather clear indications that he is ready to be converted to Bober's self-sacrificing morality. One, of course, is his return to the grocery store to assist Morris, motivated at least in part by the desire to atone. Another is his admiration for St. Francis of Assisi, who "was born good" (28). In Morris, Frank has once again found someone who "was born good" and who can thus help him find himself, his place in the world. In a commentary upon Malamud, Samuel A. Weiss has said: "Symbolically enrolled in the Jewish camp . . . are all those who through suffering have discovered their true humanity and identity." [12] Through Morris, Frank is to learn the ways of *mentshlekhkayt*, to become "enrolled in the Jewish camp," at first symbolically and, with his conversion, literally.

Despite Frank's promising attachment to the Catholic saint, and despite his claim that " 'I always liked Jews,' " the fact is that until the time of his involvement in Morris Bober's life, he had shared in a normative anti-Semitism (33). Of Helen Bober, for example, "he thought she didn't look Jewish, which was all to the good," and, at the beginning at least, he often thinks of Morris simply as "the Jew" (52). Under the influence of Morris and the grocery

12. Samuel A. Weiss, "Notes on Bernard Malamud," *Chicago Jewish Forum*, XXI (Winter, 1962–63), 157.

store, however, his personality undergoes a subtle transformation. Although he continues to steal small change from the grocery, he begins to feel a twinge of conscience, and he decides to keep track of the amount he takes, with the vague idea of restoring it at a later time. He still feels a stranger among the Bobers ("They were Jews and he was not" (72)), yet he enjoys Morris's company and begins to think about the Jews and what they represent: "That's what they live for . . . to suffer. And the one that has got the biggest pain in the gut . . . is the best Jew. No wonder they got on his nerves" (71).

In spite of the disclaimer at the end, which indicates that, at least at this point, Frank is not quite conscious of the process, this passage marks the beginning of Alpine's trial of Judaism. The trial takes the form of an informal, though not casual, examination by Alpine of Jewish Law, tradition, and morality, with the idea, perhaps only semi-conscious, that in Judaism he might find what he had long sought, the satisfaction of his "need to get out of his system all that had happened—for whatever had happened had happened wrong . . . to change his life before the smell of it suffocated him" (73). That Alpine continues to ponder the Jews and their ways becomes clear with his reaction to Raskolnikov in *Crime and Punishment*, a novel that he reads to please Helen: "Frank first had the idea that he must be a Jew and was surprised when he found he wasn't" (86).

Frank's testing of Judaism becomes fully conscious and explicit when he asks Morris what the Jews believe in, wanting to know " 'what is a Jew anyway?' " (98). The grocer's reply—" 'The important thing is the Torah. This is the Law—a Jew must believe in the Law' "—elicits the response from Alpine that Morris is not a real Jew; for he neither goes to synagogue nor eats kosher. Morris's reply, that honesty and goodness count for more than ritual observance, verbalizes his deep attachment to the code of *mentshlekhkayt* and seems to satisfy Frank, who then broaches a new subject, one to which he has been giving a great deal of thought: " 'But tell me why is it that the Jews suffer so damn much, Morris? . . . What do you suffer for, Morris?' " (99). Bober's answer is enigmatic and prophetic: " 'I suffer for you' . . . 'you suffer for me' " (99–100). The implications of this statement are both universal and particular, touching upon the reciprocal responsibility of man and man, of Jew and Gentile, and, specifically, upon the convergence of the fortunes of Frank and Morris.

After Morris dies, Frank takes over the grocery store, continues to support the grocer's family, and adopts Morris's life of suffering and *mentshlekhkayt*. Frank is a Jew in spirit now, and at the novel's end he formalizes his conversion: "One day in April Frank went to the hospital and had himself circumcised. . . . The pain enraged and inspired him. After Passover he became a Jew" (192). The conversion is a vindication for Judaism in the trial through which Frank's questioning (and Morris's suffering) has brought it, although not a victory for the orthodox religious point of view: "Frank becomes a Jew, not out of religious conviction but because he elects to be, like Morris, a good man; he elects to suffer for Morris who has suffered . . . for him." [13] However, the conversion should be construed not as a victory of Judaism over Christianity but much rather as a realization of the potential for Jewish-

13. Jonathan Baumbach, "The Economy of Love: The Novels of Bernard Malamud," *Kenyon Review*, XXV (Summer, 1963), 453.

Gentile symbiosis hinted at elsewhere in Malamud's fiction: "Frank's conversion is important because he discovers— not alone, but through another human being—a law of conduct which might give meaning to the burden of suffering, to life. As he accepts faith, he paradoxically eradicates the barriers between theologies." [14]

Malamud's novel *The Fixer*—despite its setting in twentieth-century pre-revolutionary Russia, its vastly different external plot and situation—is motivated and informed by the same concerns as is *The Assistant*. It too chronicles the testing of Jewish values and the evolution of man (whether Jew or Gentile) into *mentsh*. Solotaroff, writing well before *The Fixer* was published, has made an observation which bears upon and, to some extent, illuminates these similarities: "Malamud appears to be writing mainly about Jewishness itself as it survives from age to age and from place to place." [15] A comparison of the moral concerns of the two novels bears out Solotaroff's assertion and makes it clear that in *The Fixer*, as in *The Assistant*, Malamud is indeed "writing . . . about Jewishness itself."

Yakov Bok, the protagonist and title figure of *The Fixer*, is born Jewish, yet, like Frank Alpine, during the course of the novel he undergoes a transformation, a "conversion" to the way of life of Judaism and to the values embodied in the code of *mentshlekhkayt*. As is the case with Alpine, Yakov's conversion is precipitated by a major crisis in his life and carried out under the influence of an older man, his father-in-law, Shmuel, who from the outset is deeply committed to the life of traditional Jewish morality. While the turning point for Alpine is the crime against Morris, of

14. H. E. Francis, "Bernard Malamud's Everyman," *Midstream*, VII (Winter, 1961), 94.
15. Solotaroff, p. 90.

which he is guilty but never accused, Yakov Bok's crisis is touched off by his imprisonment for the "ritual murder" of a young Russian boy in Kiev, a crime he has not committed. This lengthy and brutal imprisonment provides the physical and psychological setting for the moral transformation of Yakov, a man who has never been especially drawn to traditional Judaism and who, in his philosophical skepticism, resembles Yasha Mazur, Singer's magician.

Indeed, there is a valid basis for comparison with Singer's novel, for Yakov Bok and Yasha Mazur bear a striking surface resemblance to each other. Both grow up within the confines of the *shtetl*, but both are dissatisfied with this existence and drawn to the life of the city—Yasha to Warsaw, Yakov Bok to Kiev. Yasha is an outsider, essentially a stranger, in the *shtetl* of Lublin, and in the same way Yakov, feeling no common bond with his fellow Jews, has divorced himself from the communal life of the *shtetl*. Eventually he makes a decision to leave, as he explains to his father-in-law, Shmuel: "The shtetl is a prison, no change from the days of Khmelnitsky. It moulders and the Jews moulder in it. Here we're all prisoners . . . (15).[16] That the resemblance between Malamud's Yakov and Singer's Yasha goes far below the surface is evidenced by the similarity of moral evolution, by the fact that Yasha, too, moves from a position of skepticism to an acceptance of the ways of God and, in his self-imprisonment, of the life of restraint and responsibility to his fellow man.

On the level of plot action Yakov's troubles, like Yasha's, are rooted in his restlessness, his need to feel the freedom of life outside the confines of the ghetto. Shmuel, who in many ways resembles Morris Bober and in fact serves as a foil and guide to Yakov, as Morris does to Frank, advises

16. Bernard Malamud, *The Fixer* (New York, 1966).

his son-in-law against leaving the *shtetl*. His advice contains an implied (and prophetic) warning: " 'What's in the world,' Shmuel said, 'is in the shtetl—people, their trials, worries, circumstances. But here at least God is with us' " (16). Yakov's reply immediately establishes him as a skeptic, a critic of God in the same sense as are Yasha Mazur and Wiesel's survivors of the holocaust, and sets the tone for the trial of Judaism and God in the novel: " 'He's with us till the Cossacks come galloping, then he's elsewhere. He's in the outhouse, that's where he is' " (16). (Note that here, and elsewhere, Malamud has Yakov use the lower-case pronoun to refer to God, either as a sign of defiance and disrespect or to denote man's moral equality with God.)

Earl Rovit has pointed to the importance of the figure of Job in the fiction of Malamud, whose "characters cry out, defy, and accept. . . ." [17] Indeed, Yakov's accusations against God (like those of Wiesel) are in the tradition of the Book of Job and thus arise from within a specifically Jewish context. The significance of Job for Malamud is brought to our attention in the contrasting attitudes of Yakov and his father-in-law. Shmuel subscribes to the position of Job: "Though he slay me, yet will I trust in Him" (211). For Yakov, on the other hand, God is guilty: "To win a lousy bet with the devil he killed off all the servants and innocent children of Job. For that alone I hate him, not to mention ten thousand pogroms" (211). Shmuel, his faith unshakable, brings to mind Nelly Sachs in his emphasis upon Job's allegiance to God, while Yakov, like Elie Wiesel, concentrates upon God's injustice and Job's defiant reaction, his rebellion against God. Their dialogue,

17. Earl H. Rovit, "Bernard Malamud and the Jewish Literary Tradition," *Critique*, III (Winter, 1960), 10.

moreover, captures the special quality of the relationship between the two men, which may be characterized as that of prophet and unwilling disciple and which is developed in some detail from the beginning of the work. This developing relationship, delineating as it does Yakov's internal struggle between defiance and acceptance, between skepticism and belief, thus serves as a vehicle for the trial of Judaism as it unfolds in the novel.

Early in the novel Yakov explains to Shmuel that he plans to leave the *shtetl* because " 'what I want to know is what's going on in the world' " (16). Shmuel's response, reflecting an unworldly naiveté, expresses a genuine Orthodox Jewish belief as well: " 'That's all in the Torah, there's no end to it. Stay away from the wrong books, Yakov, the impure' " (16). On the way to Kiev, Yakov and Shmuel (who accompanies his son-in-law to the edge of the *shtetl*) encounter a beggar asking for two kopeks. Although destitute himself, Shmuel's sense of responsibility asserts itself and he asks to borrow a few kopeks from Yakov in order to give the money to the beggar. Yakov's refusal demonstrates that the difference between the two men goes beyond questions of faith in God and acceptance of traditional Judaism, that it also involves the code of *mentshlekhkayt* in an essential way.

The final interchange between Shmuel and Yakov before Yakov's departure for Kiev reiterates their antithetical viewpoints: " 'Yakov,' said Shmuel passionately, 'don't forget your god!' 'Who forgets who?' the fixer said angrily. 'What do I get from him but a bang on the head and a stream of piss in my face. So what's there to be worshipful about?' " (20). However, at this point a new idea is introduced: " 'Don't talk like a meshummed. Stay a Jew, Yakov, don't give up our God.' 'A meshummed gives up one God for another. I don't want either' " (20). Here Yakov contrasts with Yasha Mazur, who actually did consider conversion to Christianity and even half-believed himself capable of going through with the act. Yakov's stand on this issue is especially interesting in view of his assumption of a Christian name and identity in Kiev and his undeniable attraction to Christian trappings and ritual that manifests itself once he has left the *shtetl*.

The first indication of this is Yakov's reaction to the anti-Semitic boatman, who, unaware that Yakov is a Jew, rows him across the Dnieper and vents a particularly virulent outburst in which he advocates genocide to " 'save us all from the bloody Jews,' " with " 'no exception made for young or old . . . because our Lord, who they crucified, wants his rightful revenge' " (28–29). Afterward the boatman "dropped an oar and crossed himself" and, we are told, "Yakov fought an impulse to do the same" (29). Yakov does not make the sign of the cross, but he does drop his bag with prayer book, prayer shawl, and phylacteries into the river. Once in Kiev, he visits a church, watching "from the gallery . . . as the peasants . . . knelt and prayed at the altar before a tall gold crucifix and a jeweled ikon of the Madonna, as the priest . . . chanted the Orthodox service" (31). Later he visits the Lavra catacombs, once again observing and moving among the peasants with a certain fascination. "Yakov had considered a quick kiss of the bony fingers, [but] when his time came to kneel, he blew out his candle and groped his way out in the dark" (31). Thus a pattern emerges: like Yasha Mazur, Yakov feels somehow drawn to Christianity but, as becomes increasingly clear, he is incapable of taking even the first small step toward making a commitment to it.

During his imprisonment Yakov's attachment to Juda-

ism and the Jews becomes strengthened as a natural concomitant of his conversion to the morality imposed by the
code of *mentshlekhkayt*. Thus, when somewhat later the
prosecuting attorney, Grubeshov, offers Yakov a short sentence and a quick parole in exchange for his agreement to
sign a statement implicating the "Jewish Nation" in the
murder (perhaps to be used to justify a future pogrom),
the fixer refuses. Yakov's refusal to spare himself at the expense of other innocent Jews is not completely unexpected,
in spite of his earlier anxiety to leave the *shtetl*. For, not
long before his arrest for murder, in an incident that may
in fact have led to his arrest, Yakov intervenes on behalf of
an old Hasidic Jew under attack by a group of boys; driving
the boys away, he invites the man to his room in order to
treat the wound. The invitation exposes Yakov to danger
and possible imprisonment, as Jews are legally forbidden
to reside in the district in which Yakov's room is located,
and the fixer is thus living there under false pretenses. The
act, then, reflects Yakov's courage as well as his innate
sense of responsibility to his fellow man. The old Jew refuses Yakov's offer of food, instead eating the Passover
matzos that he had brought with him. "It came as a sur-
prise to the fixer that it was Passover. He was moved by
a strong emotion and had to turn away until it had gone"
(59). Yakov's reaction here indicates that, on the level of
emotion at least, his ties to Judaism have not been completely severed and, like Alpine, he is a promising subject
for conversion to the life lived by the code of *mentshlekhkayt*.

Although Yakov's transformation doesn't involve conversion in the strict sense of the word, it nevertheless provides another example of Malamud's tendency to de-
emphasize the distinctions between Jew and Christian,

pointing to the common ethical ground shared by Judaism and true Christianity. Yakov's attraction to Christianity and simultaneous emotional attachment to Judaism have already been noted. It is significant, therefore, that the fixer's moral evolution in essence begins with his reading of the New Testament given to him secretly by the guard Zhitnyak, whose wife is concerned about saving Yakov's soul: " 'If you want to read the true word of God, read the gospels. My old woman told me to tell you that' " (189–190). Yakov is at first repelled by the notion of reading the New Testament, "having from childhood feared Jesus Christ, as stranger, apostate, mysterious enemy of the Jews" (190). Out of boredom and curiosity, however, he begins to read, finding himself fascinated by the story of Jesus and deeply moved by the Crucifixion. In a specifically Jewish (as opposed to Christian) interpretation of the Crucifixion, Yakov stresses the culpability of God, identifying Jesus with those Old Testament figures, like Job and Jeremiah, who rebuke God for the suffering of mankind, and, ultimately, with himself: "Afterwards he thought if that's how it happened and it's part of the Christian religion, and they believe it, how can they keep me in prison, knowing I am innocent" (90). Indicated here is an analogy between the code of *mentshlekhkayt* and the ethical teachings of the Christian Savior, with the further implication that the Christians have too often forgotten these teachings.

An example is Nikolai Lebedev, Yakov's employer and a member of the anti-Semitic Black Hundred. Lebedev is a pious hypocrite who cries when he reads the Sermon on the Mount and whose anti-Semitism, in his opinion, makes him a better Christian. On the other hand, there are several significant contrary examples, among them the guard Kogin and Bibikov. The latter, a morally upright man of great intelligence, becomes convinced of Yakov's innocence early in his investigation of the case. However, all his efforts on behalf of the Jew result in his own imprisonment and eventual suicide. An even more interesting case is that of Kogin, who undergoes a moral conversion which parallels that of Yakov himself. Like Bibikov, the guard ultimately gives up his life for the sake of his morality, for on the morning that Yakov is finally to go to trial there is an incident involving the deputy warden, who appears at the point of shooting the fixer. Kogin, feeling that "enough is enough," draws his gun to defend Yakov: " 'I've listened to this man night after night, I know his sorrows . . . anyway it's time for his trial to begin' " (264). Kogin fires at the ceiling and the deputy warden kills him.

If Kogin's adoption of true Christian morality brings to mind Yakov's evolution, Bibikov, an established center of morality whose wisdom and devotion to his fellow man are evident from the outset, resembles Shmuel. These similarities establish Bibikov and Kogin as examples of the fusion of Judaism with Christianity that H. E. Francis mentions in his comments upon *The Assistant*.[18] A further example is Yakov's defense attorney, Suslov-Smirnow, who "was in his youth anti-Semitic but . . . is now a vigorous defender of the rights of Jews" (253). The defense attorney exemplifies the potential of man for moral evolution, a potential whose ultimate realization by the fixer himself in my view provides the novel's principal thrust.

Yakov's moral education, having begun with his absorption in the gospels and fascination with the figure of Jesus, in the final analysis centers upon his developing relationship with Judaism and the trial to which he subjects the God of Israel. Early in his imprisonment Yakov's feelings

18. Francis, p. 94.

about God recall those that he had expressed before leaving the *shtetl*: "He sometimes thought God was punishing him for his unbelief. He was, after all, the jealous God. 'Thou shalt worship no other Gods before me,' not even no Gods" (127). And, somewhat later: "What was being a Jew but an everlasting curse? He was sick of their history, destiny, blood guilt" (187). Nevertheless, that a change is gradually manifesting itself becomes evident when a fanatical priest attempts to persuade the Jew to confess, repent, and convert to the (Russian) Orthodox faith. With the approach of the priest, Yakov seeks refuge in Jewish ritual: "Yakov stood in the dim light, motionless at the table, the prayer shawl covering his head, the phylactery for the arm bound to his brow" (194).

After the visit of the priest Yakov's New Testament is confiscated and an Old Testament in Hebrew is thrown into the cell by the deputy warden. In spite of the fact that half of the pages are missing, the fixer is ". . . gripped by the narrative of the joyous and frenzied Hebrews . . . always engaged in talk with the huffing-puffing God who tried to sound, maybe out of envy, like a human being" (196). Yakov begins to consider God in new terms, no longer merely expressing skepticism and blaming God for the suffering of the Jews: "God talks. He has chosen, he says, the Hebrews to preserve him. He covenants, therefore he is. He offers and Israel accepts. . . . But Israel accepts the covenant in order to break it. That's the mysterious purpose: they need the experience" (196). Imprisonment leaves Yakov with time to read and think, and he reaches new insights concerning Judaism and God's relationship with the Jews: "The purpose of the covenant, Yakov thinks, is to create human experience, although human experience baffles God" (197).

Bernard Malamud

123

The fixer's moral-religious growth is decisively furthered by his relationship with Shmuel, which reasserts its influence when the older man spends forty rubles and risks his life to visit Yakov in prison. The hurried conversation between the two bears all the earmarks of their past religious discussions. Once again Shmuel insists that "without the covenant [the Jews] would have disappeared out of history" (210). And although he recognizes the persecution to which the Jew has always been subject, he refuses to blame God for man's misery. Against Shmuel's arguments, grounded in traditional Jewish thought, Yakov, remindful of Yasha Mazur, counterposes the philosophy of Spinoza, whose life and work have long interested him and who "represents a liberation from the traditional Jewish God which is still profoundly Jewish." [19]

It is only later, after the excitement of the visit has receded somewhat, that Yakov begins to grasp the truth of Shmuel's message, whose real meaning lies not so much in theological argument but rather in the example set by Shmuel's life, by his unfailing adherence to the code of *mentshlekhkayt*. The fixer dreams that the old man is dead and, upon awakening, he realizes that his own suffering is not without meaning: " 'Live, Shmuel,' he sighs, 'live. Let me die for you! . . . if I must suffer let it be for something. Let it be for Shmuel' " (222). Yakov's relationship to his own Jewishness and to the Jews has now evolved to the point that ". . . he believes in their right to be Jews and live in the world like men. . . . This is his covenant with himself. If God's not a man he has to be" (222–223).

Yakov's formulation here, remarkably similar to the ulti-

19. Gabriel Pearson, "Bellow, Malamud, and Jewish Arrival," in Murray Mindlin, ed., *Explorations* (London, 1967), p. 28.

mate insights achieved by Singer's Yasha Mazur and Wiesel's Gregor/Gavriel of *The Gates of the Forest,* is more
than a theoretical explanation of the suffering he has been
made to endure, for it contains the germ of a plan of action
as well: ". . . he must endure to the trial and let them
confirm his innocence by their lies" (223). The Jewish
lawyer, Julius Ostrovsky, speaks for the Jews of Russia
when he tells Yakov, " 'You suffer for us all,' " but the
fixer's final understanding of the responsibilities imposed
upon him by the code of *mentshlekhkayt* reaches beyond
Ostrovsky's frame of reference:

> "I don't want to eat," said the fixer, "I want to fast."
> "What the hell for?" said Kogin.
> *"For God's world."*
> "I thought you didn't believe in God."
> "I don't." [247, 261; italics mine.]

Yakov's words make it clear that no theological conversion has taken place; indeed, the novel's end finds him still
unprepared to accept the Hebraic "talking God." Rather,
his conversion, like Shmuel's message, centers on standards
of morality, on his attitude and behavior toward his fellow
man. With the broadening of Yakov's perspective, with
the extension of the range of his self-imposed sense of responsibility (he is at first responsible for Shmuel, then for
all of the Jews, finally "for God's world"), his moral conversion, the evolution into *mentsh*, has been completed.
The true significance of Yakov's personal triumph, in his
surviving of unspeakable physical and psychological op-
pression finally to win the right to a trial, resides precisely
in that in so doing he has transcended his own skepticism
and the deficiencies of his nature to discover the ways of
mentshlekhkayt. Yakov's skepticism has put God on trial

and tested Judaic doctrine; his ultimate acceptance of the uniquely Jewish moral code, despite a continued refusal to accept the Jewish God, demonstrates Yakov's absorption of the moral message of the Old Testament and, in the final analysis, justifies Judaism.

SIX

Jewish America: Saul Bellow

The fictional world of Saul Bellow has often been discussed from the point of view of its relationship to the works of Roth and Malamud. Indeed, despite obvious differences of technique and tone, these three Jewish-American novelists do display a certain unanimity of concern for the dualism and moral tension inherent in Jewish life in America.[1] Perhaps less obvious are the points of contact between the fictional concerns of Bellow and those of Elie Wiesel.

As we have indicated earlier, Wiesel's *The Gates of the Forest* achieves an affirmation (albeit a tenuous and difficult one) based upon Hasidic mysticism, as does his more recent novel, *A Beggar in Jerusalem*.[2] Significantly, Wiesel has chosen the Hasidic masters as the subject of the collection of stories issued under the title *Souls on Fire*. In these Hasidic portraits Wiesel presents a unifying theme, the common belief of the masters that man can attain perfection, that man has within him the possibility of compassion and hope, pride, love, and humility.

1. See, for example, Theodore Solotaroff, "Philip Roth and the Jewish Moralists," *Chicago Review*, XIII (Winter, 1959), 92.
2. See the review of Wiesel's *Souls on Fire* by Charles Silverman, *New York Times Book Review* (Mar. 7, 1972), p. 1. It is interesting that Silverman observes the connection between Wiesel and Camus, a connection that I explore in "Wiesel and the Absurd," *Wisconsin Studies in Contemporary Literature* (Spring, 1974).

Though Saul Bellow is a writer very different from Wiesel, it has been written of him that "Bellow's basic attitudes— the overwhelming need for love and the joy in life—bear a remarkable similarity to the principles of Hasidism. . . . He is a secular hasid." [3] The contrast with Wiesel, who is by no means "secular," is evident. Nevertheless, the basic principle remains that Bellow, like Wiesel, is drawn into the ambience of Jewish history, which finds expression, directly and indirectly, in his fiction. Nowhere in Bellow's work is this more evident than in his latest novel, *Mr. Sammler's Planet*, and its predecessor, *Herzog*, but the concern with a Jewish morality, with the Jewish role within a larger society, was already established in the earlier novels.

This is true in particular of *The Victim*, which deals with the complex relationship between the protagonist, the Jewish Asa Leventhal, and his non-Jewish antagonist, Kirby Allbee. After a lengthy period during which the two men have not seen each other, a down-at-the-heels Allbee one day appears to confront and accuse Leventhal; Allbee holds Leventhal responsible for his downfall, beginning with the loss of his job, which he attributes to an argument between Leventhal and his former employer, Rudiger. Leventhal responds at first with complete denial of responsibility in the matter, attributing Allbee's difficulties to excessive drinking rather than to the disagreement between himself and Rudiger. Soon, however, Leventhal begins to fluctuate between anger and pity, especially when he learns that Allbee's wife left him and later died: "He was her husband. . . . He has to be considered. She's dead, but he's alive and feels. That's what brought him down. He wouldn't be like

3. Chester E. Eisinger, *Fiction of the Forties* (Chicago, 1963), p. 343.

this otherwise" (71).[4] Later Leventhal questions his own innocence, half-believing the accusation that he provoked Rudiger into a disagreement in order to discredit Allbee, who had arranged the meeting as a favor to Asa. Leventhal's growing sense of guilt is, in part, a response to the demands of the code of *mentshlekhkayt*; although the affair with Allbee "was, after all, something he could either take seriously or dismiss as an annoyance," he is unable to reconcile dismissal of the matter with his conscience (91). He feels responsible for Allbee, just as in his brother's absence he feels committed to care for his brother's family: ". . . he liked to think that 'human' meant accountable" (139). As in Wiesel's Jewish victims of the Nazis, Leventhal's adherence to a moral code, his sense of responsibility toward other men, increases his susceptibility to victimization. Allbee, sensing this, does manage to victimize Leventhal, keeping him off balance and forcing concessions from him. Just as important, on the other hand, is Leventhal's real involvement, no matter how peripheral, in Allbee's downfall. Thus Leventhal's sense of guilt is based, at least in part, upon his dual role as victim and victimizer; Bellow is not "content with the simple equation: the victim equals the Jew, the Jew the victim."[5] Indeed, Leslie Fiedler points to the fact that "Bellow alone among our novelists has had the imagination and the sheer nerve to portray the Jew, the Little Jew, as victimizer as well as victim."[6] Thus, like Wiesel in *Dawn* and *Town beyond the Wall*, Bellow in *The Victim* carries out an exploration of the ambiguities in the relationship between victim and executioner, which

4. Saul Bellow, *The Victim* (New York, 1947).
5. Leslie Fiedler, "Saul Bellow," *Prairie Schooner*, XXXI (Summer, 1957), 102.
6. *Ibid.*, p. 107.

serves both as philosophical underpinning and as a focus of plot development and characterization within the novel.

The question of Leventhal's Jewishness emerges as a concern central to the novel, insofar as his attitude and behavior toward Allbee are strongly influenced by the code of *mentshlekhkayt,* and since Allbee, in turn, exhibits a certain normative anti-Semitism: "You Jews have funny ideas about drinking. Especially the one that all Gentiles are born drunkards" (38). (Leventhal, Allbee feels, intentionally caused him trouble in order to get even, because "you were sore at something I said about Jews" (38).) Leventhal "is uncertain of what it means to be a Jew, because he does not know yet what it is to be a man"; thus, while testing his manhood, Leventhal's confrontation with Allbee simultaneously puts his Jewishness on trial, challenging his ability to be a *mentsh,* to act according to the Jewish moral code under difficult circumstances.[7] That Leventhal feels constrained to take Allbee's challenge seriously is in some measure an indication of the strength of his attachment to that code.

If it is true that at the time of its publication *The Victim* was "Bellow's most specifically Jewish book," that appellation must now certainly be reserved for *Herzog,* in which many of the same concerns operative in the earlier novel are explored once again and developed more fully.[8] *Herzog* is "a novel of ancient belief tested against modernism," a work in which Judaism as a framework for viewing the world is challenged, put on trial, by the intellect of Moses Herzog.[9] Herzog's testing of Judaism as a guide to living and as a

7. *Ibid.,* pp. 106–107.
8. *Ibid.,* p. 107.
9. Melvin H. Bernstein, "Jewishness, Judaism and the American-Jewish Novelist," *Chicago Jewish Forum,* XXIII (Summer, 1965), 275–282.

moral force in the modern world is reminiscent of Alpine's examination of Judaism in *The Assistant,* despite the striking contrasts between Malamud's somewhat unschooled convert to Judaism and Bellow's intellectually powerful protagonist. Common to the two men is a deep and passionate morality which provides a unifying bond, in the long run overshadowing their great differences of style and background.

Though he is an American, Herzog's roots lay in the Eastern European *shtetl* of Singer and Wiesel, having been transplanted to the New World by his immigrant parents. Herzog is "a good man . . . a good heart," and, like his mother, "a gentle spirit" (139).[10] Responsive to the Commandments, Herzog worships his father as "a sacred being, a king. . . . Whom did I ever love as I loved them?" (147). The richness and color of the immigrant urban experience have had a profound effect upon Herzog's personality, and it is within this context that his attachment to the Jewish past ("My ancient times. Remoter than Egypt") has been shaped: "Napolean Street, rotten, toylike, crazy and filthy . . . the bootlegger's boys reciting ancient prayers. To this Moses' heart was attached with great power. Here was a wider range of human feelings than he had ever again been able to find" (140).

But, reaching beyond his own past to links with the historical fortunes of the Jewish people, Herzog feels endowed with a Jewish historical consciousness, a Jungian "racial memory"; he senses direct, personal access to ancient Jewish experience as well as recent events of Jewish history from which he was physically far removed:

> So we had a great schooling in grief. I still know these cries
> of the soul. . . . But all these are antiquities—yes, Jewish

10. Saul Bellow, *Herzog* (New York, 1964).

antiquities originating in the Bible, in a Biblical sense of
personal experience and destiny. What happened during
the War abolished Father Herzog's claim to exceptional suffering. We are on a more brutal standard now, a new termi-
nal standard, indifferent to persons. . . . I remember. I
must. But who else—to whom can this matter? So many
millions—multitudes—go down in terrible pain. [148-149]

As with Wiesel's victims of the holocaust, who seek survival only to keep alive the memory of the event, to remain
as witnesses, Herzog "persecuted everyone" with the power
of his memory, which "was like a terrible engine" (132).
To Herzog, memory is less a blessing than a curse which
forces upon him the custody of "all the dead and mad,"
making him "the nemesis of the would-be forgotten" (134).
    Herzog is haunted as well by his inability to escape from
the responsibilities imposed by the code of *mentshlekhkayt*,
which emerges as the moral standard against which people
in the novel are judged, not only by Herzog but by those
who often do not themselves adhere to the code. Sandor
Himmelstein, for example, no model of moral rectitude
himself, praises Herzog as "A human being! A *mensch!*":
"You're a real, genuine old Jewish type that digs the emotions. . . . I understand it. I grew up . . . when a Jew
was still a Jew" (82, 84). It is true, as Himmelstein suggests, that Herzog's moral sense is intimately bound to the
emotions, to his concern for the "range of human feelings."
That Herzog openly, indiscriminately, displays his emotions, to his own detriment, becomes clear from a description of his familial attachments: "Moses loved his relatives
quite openly and even helplessly. . . . It was childish of
him; he knew that" (78). Indeed, the surrender to emotion
is (as it is for Leventhal) at the root of Herzog's victimization by people and events, against which he is determined

to struggle: "I'm not going to be a victim. I hate the victim bit" (82). On the other hand, the power of Herzog's intellect elevates his moral sensibility beyond the merely nostalgic or emotional to do battle against what he terms "the commonplaces of the Wasteland outlook, the cheap mental stimulants of Alienation" (75). It is from within this context that Herzog silently rebukes his old friend, Shapiro, for putting forth "a merely aesthetic critique of modern history! After the wars and mass killings! You are too intelligent for this. You inherited rich blood. Your father peddled apples" (75).

The ironic juxtaposition Bellow employs here reveals within Herzog a capacity to apply even nostalgia to the purposes of his purely rational discourse against alienation and nihilism, against "the canned sauerkraut of Spengler's 'Prussian Socialism' . . . the cant and rant of pipsqueaks about Inauthenticity and Forlornness" (74–75). This discourse, Herzog's struggle against the modern-day collapse of humanism, is carried forward by means of silent one-way disputation with the great (and not so great) seminal thinkers of modern Western civilization and, in the ancient Hebrew tradition, with God himself. The dispute develops into a kind of internal plot within the novel, ultimately assuming an importance equal to that of the external one, which chronicles the difficulties in Herzog's private life, the breakup of his two marriages, the unfaithfulness of his neurotic second wife, Madelaine, and of his friend, Gerspach.

The internal plot emerges as a vehicle for testing the viability of ancient Jewish values, deriving from the sacred writings and giving rise to the code of *mentshlekhkayt*, by opposing these values to "the new attitude which makes life a trifle not worth anyone's anguish" (272). It is in this sense that *Herzog* carries out the trial of Judaism. Herzog's "defense of man" (to borrow John Clayton's phrase) [11] against "the Wasteland outlook" rests finally upon that Hasidic affirmation often noted by critics of Bellow: "Let life continue—we may not deserve it, but let it continue" (51). This attachment to the Hasidic ideal is not confined to the level of intellect alone but is reflected in Herzog's actions as well. "It was one of his oddities," for example, "in solitude to break out in song and dance, to do queer things out of keeping with his customary earnestness" (158).

Concomitant with Herzog's celebration of life is an affirmation of society that entails the principal tenets of the code of *mentshlekhkayt*, the importance of community and mutual responsibility among men: "I really believe that brotherhood is what makes a man human. . . . The real and essential question is one of our employment by other human beings and their employment by us" (272). Thus, along with the Hasidic "inspired condition," in *Herzog* Bellow presents a case for "social service, [for] finding . . . salvation in a practical, hard-headed manhood," combining "the reliance on an inner vision and the determination to act in the social or external world." [12] In Keith Opdahl's view Herzog's union of "the internal and the external . . . creates . . . the chief difficulty in the novel." [13] On the other hand, as a counter to that terrible failure of the human spirit leading to the holocaust, Herzog himself argues for the inevitability, perhaps even the necessity, of such a union: "The practical questions have thus become the ul-

11. John J. Clayton, *Saul Bellow: In Defense of Man* (Bloomington, Ind., 1968).

12. Keith Opdahl, *The Novels of Saul Bellow: An Introduction* (University Park, Pa., 1967), p. 141.

13. *Ibid.*

timate questions as well. Annihilation is no longer a meta-
phor. Good and Evil are real. The inspired condition is
therefore no visionary matter. It . . . belongs to mankind
and to all of existence" (165).

Herzog thus expresses the peculiarly Jewish belief that the
strength of a man's virtue and spiritual capacity can and
should be measured by the ordinary affairs of his life, the
traditional attitude that "the duty of the Jew is to lift up
all of life to God, *to hallow the everyday*, so that all of life
becomes holy." [14] This emphasis upon what might be
termed "the sanctification of the mundane" is especially
prominent in Hasidic Judaism, which John Clayton identifies as an essential feature of "Bellow's cultural context." [15]
That the Jew "has been conscious of the presence of an
ideal world lying not outside but within the everyday world"
begins to explain how he has often remained essentially op-
timistic and affirmative, even "in the face of the grimmest
facts," how and why the Jewish community, faced with its
extermination during the holocaust, nevertheless clung to
the code of *mentshlekhkayt*.[16]

This uniquely Jewish view of life serves to explain
Herzog's difficult but triumphant optimism. It also provides
an interesting perspective from which to consider Rovit's
opinion of Bellow as a writer of "lesser stature" when compared with Faulkner and Hemingway, who were "capable of
rejecting or ignoring the world in order to construct their
own worlds. . . . Their majesty consists in their ability to
have built counterworlds. . . ." [17] Rovit observes that Bel-

14. Samuel H. Dresner, *The Jewish Dietary Laws* (New York,
1959), p. 17.
15. Clayton, Chapter 2, especially pp. 31–33.
16. *Ibid.*, p. 31.
17. Earl H. Rovit, "Bellow in Occupancy," in Irving Malin, ed.,
Saul Bellow and the Critics (New York, 1967), p. 182.

low cannot do this and concludes that he "may conceivably surrender too much of his private myth to the exigencies of the world." [18] However, in looking at the question from the perspective of Jewish tradition, one may draw a conclusion of quite another sort: that in structuring his outlook to correspond with the world as he finds it, Bellow is responding to Judaic world-rootedness, that he is therefore a profoundly "Jewish" writer, and, finally, that Bellow's fictional world is of necessity quite different in kind from that of either Faulkner or Hemingway. The fact of this difference, it seems to me, does not in itself bear upon the question of Bellow's stature relative to other significant writers of fiction, but rather it has implications for the point of view one should adopt in attempting to understand and judge his work. It appears to reflect one of Bellow's strengths, for example, that "for Herzog a new life means not removal from the brutal and mediocre stages of life but reconciliation with them." [19]

In fact, the end of *Herzog* finds the external circumstances of the protagonist's life very much the same as at the novel's opening. His personal life remains fragmented, complicated; serious work on his part seems to be out of the question; his financial position is precarious, as is his relationship with Ramona. Yet his internal emotional state has altered significantly, and for the first time he appears to be capable of accepting the situation in which he finds himself: "I am pretty well satisfied to be, to be just as it is willed and for as long as I may remain in occupancy" (340). Most significant is the cessation of that compulsive writing of unmailed letters to famous personages of the past and

18. *Ibid.*
19. Ronald Weber, "Bellows Thinkers," *Western Humanities Review*, XXII (1968), 311.

present, to personal friends and enemies, which had provided the *modus operandi* within the novel for the testing of Herzog's Jewish moral stance in the arena of contemporary society. When at the end of the novel Herzog realizes "that he [is] done with these letters," he also understands the deeper implications of this fact: "At this time he had no messages for anyone. Nothing. Not a single word" (341).

Thus, with the end of the novel, Herzog's trial of Judaism ends as well; that the result of the trial is to be an affirmative one for the Jewish moral outlook becomes increasingly clear as the work unfolds, unraveling with it the "Jewish mind" of Moses Herzog (106). From the outset it is clear that Herzog's ethical sense is a distinctly Jewish one, responding to the code of *mentshlekhkayt*. But it soon becomes evident that, despite his skeptical intellectualism, Herzog has a profound store of religious feelings as well. As with Singer's Yasha Mazur, Herzog's skepticism yields to a deeper, somewhat mystical, religious sense in response to the marvels of nature: "The lawn was on an elevation with a view of fields and woods. . . . An oriole's nest, in the shape of a gray heart, hung from twigs. God's veil over things makes them all riddles" (72). Though Herzog reveals some astonishment at his attachment to God ("Evidently I continue to believe in God. Though never admitting it" (231)), the strength of this attachment occasionally overwhelms him, forcing itself to his consciousness among other, apparently unrelated thoughts: "Dear Ramona, I owe you a lot. I am fully aware of it. Though I may not be coming back to New York right away, I intend to keep in touch. Dear God! Mercy! My God! . . . Thou King of Death and Life . . . !" (304). Evidently for Moses Herzog the intention "to keep in touch" carries with it the resolve not to forget his boyhood, his early life lived under the influence of the God of Israel and his commandments.

Herzog, like Wiesel's protagonists, struggles against these early influences, putting God himself on trial, citing the evidence of history and, in particular, of "these millions of dead" (290). The enormities of the holocaust lead Herzog to the conclusion that "if the old God exists he must be a murderer" (290). The formulation "God is dead" is no longer operative; according to Herzog, "that point was passed by long ago. Perhaps it should be stated Death is God" (290). Herzog thus rises against God, but, in contrast to Gregor of *The Town beyond the Wall*, he finds it impossible to sustain the rebellion, instead declaring his acceptance of the God of Israel in the traditional formulation of the Old Testament patriarchs: ". . . here I am. *Hineni*. How marvelously beautiful is today" (310). Gregor accepts Hasidic Judaism while continuing to question God; Herzog, by contrast, accepts the Jewish God without accepting Judaism in a theological sense. For Bellow's protagonist, indeed, involvement with Judaism means primarily acceptance of the moral code of *mentshlekhkayt* and recognition of the Jewish historical consciousness.

Significantly, Herzog's final letter is addressed to God; in it he writes that his "mind has struggled to make coherent sense," but he confesses his failure as well as his desire "to do your unknowable will, taking it, and you, without symbols" (325–326). But for Herzog, as for Singer's Yasha, submission to God's will is alloyed with lingering doubts, historically justified, about the justice of God's ways toward mankind. Thus, though the writing of *Herzog* may indeed constitute a "modern effort to justify God's ways to man," as Rovit has claimed, the effort is not wholly successful.[20] For, simply put, acceptance is not justification. Despite Herzog's insistence upon life's intrinsic value and beauty in the face of "the wars and mass killings," which parallels

20. Rovit, p. 178.

Wiesel's resolution of the philosophical-theological problems raised in *The Gates of the Forest*, Bellow, like Wiesel,
recognizes the grave difficulties inhering in this resolution:
"I don't pretend that my position . . . is easy. We are survivors. . . . To realize that you are a survivor is a shock. At
the realization of such election, you feel like bursting into
tears. As the dead go their way, you want to call to them,
but they depart in a black cloud of faces, souls. They flow
out in smoke from the extermination chimneys . . ." (75).
Thus, though there is truth in Opdahl's claim that "religious insight in Bellow's fiction requires the hero to surrender to God," the surrender is not complete; in *Herzog* it
is tempered by a persistent cognizance of the Jewish catastrophe that is the holocaust.[21]

Despite the fact that Herzog, an American, has not himself lived through the holocaust, he nevertheless "experiences" the catastrophe, making genuine contact in terms of
his profound sense of racial identification, through his involvement with the history of the Jewish people. The events
of the Nazi period in Europe engage his historian's mind, as
they do the philosophical-theological aspect of his nature.
Thus it is not surprising that as a visitor to Warsaw Herzog
"went many times to visit the ruins of the ghetto" (25).
However, for Herzog the holocaust experience of necessity
remains somewhat remote, something of a mental construct. With *Mr. Sammler's Planet* Bellow confronts the
reader more directly with the destruction of European
Jewry, for Artur Sammler, now over seventy, is himself a
survivor of the extermination camps. Sammler's wife was a
victim of the Nazis and he has escaped death himself only
through a lucky chance and his ability to survive extreme
hardship and deprivation. Thus in Sammler we are confronted with a "survivor" in a stricter sense than that in

21. Opdahl, p. 26.

which the term might apply to Herzog. In this respect, indeed, Arthur Sammler is more akin to Wiesel's protagonists than he is to Herzog.

If, as has been asserted, "Leventhal, as victim, is but a simplification of Herzog as victim," it is equally true that Sammler as victim represents an intensification of Herzog as victim.[22] As in *The Victim* and the novels of Wiesel, the role of victim in *Mr. Sammler's Planet* is an ambiguous one, the distinction between victim and executioner often blurring. Two incidents in the work particularly point to this. In the first of these Sammler, having miraculously escaped death at the hands of the Germans by crawling out of a mass grave, has become a partisan in the Zamosht Forest. There he unhesitatingly shoots a German soldier, ignoring the man's pleas for mercy. Especially significant are Sammler's later reflections upon this incident; he has come to realize "that to kill the man he ambushed in the snow had give him pleasure. . . . It was joy" (140).[23] Furthermore, killing the German, "Sammler, himself nearly a corpse, burst into life" (140). This reaction contrasts dramatically with that of Wiesel's Elisha in *Dawn*, who considers his execution of an English officer to be tantamount to an act of self-destruction: "That's it. . . . It's done. I've killed. I've killed Elisha." [24] It contrasts as well with the behavior of Herzog, who briefly, somewhat comically, contemplates shooting his former wife, Madelaine, and her lover but quickly makes the same discovery as does Singer's Yasha Mazur—that, as has been clear to the reader from the outset, a criminal act would be inimical to his nature.

The second episode involves Eisen, estranged husband of

22. Dudley Flamm, "Herzog—Victim and Hero," *Zeitschrift für Anglistik und Amerikanistik*, XVII, no. 2 (1969), 174–188.

23. Saul Bellow, *Mr. Sammler's Planet* (New York, 1970).

24. Elie Wiesel, *Dawn* (New York, 1961), p. 89.

Sammler's daughter, Shula, and a black pickpocket whose activities Sammler has been regularly observing in fascination while riding the bus. In a public altercation on the streets of New York City, Eisen, a survivor of the holocaust and victim of Russian anti-Semitism, comes close to killing the black man. He is prevented from crushing the man's skull only by the intervention of Sammler, who is "horrified" by the incident. Eisen's retort is especially telling in the light of Sammler's own past: "You can't hit a man like this just once. When you hit him you must really hit him. Otherwise he'll kill you. You know. We both fought in the war. You were a Partisan. You had a gun. So don't you know?" (291). The ironic content of Eisen's argument has a profound effect upon his father-in-law ("It was the reasoning that sank Sammler's heart completely" (292)), who unquestionably is reminded at this point of his German victim.

The two incidents, separated by some thirty years of time as well as great differences of setting and circumstances, are not strictly comparable. Nevertheless, the contrast in Sammler's behavior at these two points in his life does help to bring into focus the Jewish context within which the moral-religious development of his later years takes place. To understand this development, it is of course necessary to consider Sammler's earlier years, concerning which the old man reveals that he "didn't have much to do with the synagogue. We were almost freethinkers. Especially my mother. She had a Polish education. She gave me an emancipated name: Artur" (84). Thus, though it is a temptation to think of Sammler as an "older Herzog"—and there is in fact some validity in this analogy, notably the similar sense of history and intense intellectualism of the two men—there is a critical difference in background. Herzog, like

Wiesel's protagonist, is a product of that Jewish pietism associated to a large extent with the *shtetl* culture of Eastern Europe, while Sammler's family have joined the intellectual mainstream of modern Western civilization. The difference in background gives rise to an essential difference in moral stance as well, for Sammler is unfettered by that unyielding, apparently unreasonable, adherence to God's commandments that characterizes Wiesel's unresisting victims of the holocaust. While it would be speculative to conclude that Herzog would not have killed the German quite so freely as did Sammler (if at all), the analogy with Wiesel's protagonist at least provides some evidence for such speculation.

Having taken a man's life, Sammler engages in some speculation of his own: "He would have thanked God for this opportunity. If he had had any God. At that time, he did not. For many years, in his own mind, there was no judge but himself" (141). In contrast to the young Eliezer of *Night*, who puts God on trial as a desperate expression of betrayed, disappointed faith but is unable to reject that faith, Sammler, confronting the holocaust, revolts against God by suspending entirely a belief that was perhaps never an essential part of his being.

However, years later in New York City, faced once again with suffering, this time that of Walter Bruch, Sammler astonishes Bruch, and the reader as well, with the response: " 'I'll pray for you, Walter' " (63). The incredulous Bruch reacts with laughter, but Sammler, unyielding, once more repeats the promise to pray for him. The profound change in Sammler's religious views revealed in this interchange is a significant indication of the general development in Sammler's personality that has taken place since the end of the war and his arrival in New York. As Sammler himself puts it, he hadn't really survived the holocaust, "since so much of the earlier person had disappeared. It wasn't surviving, it was only lasting. He had lasted" (91). The older Sammler is concerned, as the young man was not, with his "God adumbrations in the many daily forms"; he "very often, and almost daily [has] strong impressions of eternity"; he is "eaten by a longing for sacredness" and "given to praying . . . often addressed God" (237, 92, 200). Thus the Sammler who saves the black pickpocket from violence, the Sammler of New York City, is radically different, at least in moral terms, from the partisan who had taken human life long before in Poland.

The episode involving the black man intrudes upon Sammler's harried trip to the hospital to visit his critically ill nephew, Elya Gruner. The fear, later justified, that his arrival will be too late adds to Sammler's sense of desperation as he attempts to deal with Eisen's attack upon the man: "Damn these—these *occasions* . . . it was Elya who needed him" (292). It was Elya, a wealthy physician, who had brought Sammler to New York shortly after the close of the war. Gruner, motivated by "Old World family feelings," had located Artur and Shula Sammler after studying the refugee lists in the Yiddish newspapers and continued to support them financially "for twenty-two years . . . with kindness . . . without a day of neglect, without a single irascible word" (11, 215). Gruner's behavior toward the Sammlers is by no means an isolated instance. Indeed, Elya is drawn to Israel, where there "were more old relatives like Sammler, and Gruner did genealogies with them, one of his favorite pastimes. More than a pastime" (82).

Gruner, in contrast to Sammler and to his German-Jewish wife (now deceased), is an "*Ostjude* . . . the expressive one, the one with the heart," the product of an

Orthodox Jewish home, in background and emotional sensibility quite similar to Herzog (302). Indeed, if Sammler appears to be the "mature Herzog" in terms of the intellect, Gruner may be given this same label with respect to the emotional life, particularly in view of his very strong familial ties. While by no means a religious Jew, Gruner, like Herzog, is an adherent of the Jewish moral code of *mentshlekhkayt*, "a dependable man—a man who took thought for others," in Sammler's view (85). Adhering to the best in the tradition of *mentshlekhkayt*, Gruner shuns the credit for his acts of generosity: "Undisclosed charities were his pleasure. He had many stratagems of benevolence" (283). In this context it is significant that, faced in the hospital with Sammler's assertion of his goodness, "Gruner neither acknowledged nor denied this. Perhaps by the rigidity of his posture he fended off gratitude he did not deserve in full" (85).

Both Sammler and Gruner resemble Herzog in their attachment to history, to ancient times, but, curiously, they differ strikingly from each other in this respect. Again the dichotomy is one of intellect and emotion, two elements of personality which are united in the person of Herzog. Thinking of the past in terms of "the historical memory of mankind," expressing "his views—historical, planetary, and universal," Sammler displays a mature form of Herzog's astonishing intellectual capacities and interests (62, 247). By contrast, Gruner's interest in the past is primarily on an emotional level, an expression of his sentimentality, of tribal attachments, of his "passion for kinship" (82).

Though older, Sammler is easily the more forward-looking and insightful of the two men. Indeed, there is a note of criticism in his view of Gruner as "a sentimental person. He makes a point, too much of a point, of treasuring certain old feelings. He's on an old system. . . . I never had much natural liking for people who make open declarations of affection" (302). However, the operative word here is the adjective "natural"; Sammler, in fact, admires his nephew deeply on moral grounds, in spite of his natural inclination. Comparing himself with Gruner, Sammler brings Elya's highly developed moral sensibility into focus while at the same time commenting upon his own failures as a *mentsh:*

> "He did what he disliked. . . . He knew there had been good men before him, that there were good men to come, and he wanted to be one of them. I think he did all right. I don't come out nearly so well myself. Till forty or so I was simply an Anglophile intellectual Polish Jew and person of culture—relatively useless. But Elya, by sentimental repetition and by formulas if you like . . . has accomplished something good." [303]

Like Herzog, Elya felt compelled to "complete his assignment, whatever that was" (*Herzog*, 231). Thus, though Gruner "didn't like surgery . . . [and] . . . dreaded those three- and four-hour operations . . . he performed them" (*Planet*, 303).

There is, therefore, more than a little irony in the rootlessness of Elya's children, who somehow fail to come to grips with responsibility, to find their "assignments," in Bellow's term. Bellow describes Wallace Gruner, in his late twenties, with the rather humorous cataloging of an unproductive career: "Wallace nearly became a physicist, nearly became a mathematician, nearly a lawyer . . . nearly an engineer, nearly a Ph.D. in behavioral science. . . . Nearly an alcoholic, nearly a homosexual" (88). Angela is in her thirties, unmarried, given to sexual adventures.

She "sent money to defense funds for black murderers and rapists" (11). Sammler's familiarity with Angela's grandparents and their adherence to Orthodox Judaism "gave a queer edge to his acquaintance with her paganism" (72). Sharing Portnoy's perception of the effects of the Jewish milieu upon sexual response, without necessarily sharing Portnoy's negative response toward these effects, Sammler "doubted the fitness of these Jews for this erotic Roman voodoo primitivism. He questioned whether release from long Jewish mental discipline, hereditary training in lawful control, was obtainable upon individual application" (72–73).

Neither Wallace nor Angela has Elya's interest in the past, in family connections. Wallace attempts to rationalize his lack of interest in "roots" by articulating his rather general speculations upon the development of society: " 'Roots are not modern. That's a peasant conception, soil and roots. Peasantry is going to disappear. That's the real meaning of the modern revolution . . .' " (245–246). A concomitant of Wallace's rejection of the past is his alienation from religion. Confronted by the Hebrew inscriptions on Eisen's medallions, he asks a naive and somewhat irreverent question: " 'Why does God speak such a funny language?' " (170). Yet this question, coming from a man of Wallace's obvious intelligence, reveals more than naiveté or irreverence. It exposes, in fact, rejection of Judaism and God through indifference. Wallace, displaying a great interest in his father's accumulated weath but showing no tendency to emulate Elya where morality is concerned, stands, like many of Philip Roth's Jewish figures, as a rebuke to the Jewish community from which he emerges.

The possibility that Wallace may be intended as a rebuke to his father as well is an interesting one in the light of Elya's role as *mentsh*. Significantly, Wallace is preoccupied throughout the novel with a continuing search for a large cache of money he believes his father has earned illegally through Mafia connections and then hidden in the old house he owns in New Rochelle. In his inept search for the money Wallace breaks a large water pipe and causes extensive water damage to his father's house, an episode to which the obvious symbolic meaning may be attached. His suspicions appear for some time to be supported only by his own overworked imagination but are confirmed at the novel's end with the discovery of the money in the house. It is difficult either to take Gruner's illegal activities into account in assessing his character or to estimate their precise impact upon Wallace. For, whatever Elya's transgressions, they do not occur explicitly in the novel, nor is the reader supplied with more than a few vague hints concerning "some operations" (311). Wallace assumes that they were performed "as a favor to highly placed people. . . . Only out of pity" (101). Though Elya's "crimes" are without victims and appear to arise from his inability to refuse help to his friends, one may nevertheless surmise that Wallace's certainty of his father's involvement with the Mafia has had a more than negligible effect upon the young man and is indeed the source, at least in part, of his alienation from the ethical outlook of his father.

Wallace's business and professional enterprises, all dismal failures, the counterparts of his sister's unhappy sexual involvements, demonstrate an unwillingness or inability on his part to cope with the world's realities. Displaying the *shlemiel*'s somewhat comical propensity for absurd schemes and inevitable failure, and apparently without interest in the spiritual side of man's nature, Wallace offers a striking contrast both to his father and to Sammler. One has the

clear impression that Wallace lacks the basic thoughtful-
ness and moral fiber of the young Sammler, that his deep-
rooted inability to deal seriously with serious questions
would render him incapable of producing the kind of creative religious transformation that Sammler has managed in
his later years.

"In his seventies," we are told, Sammler "was interested
in little more than Meister Eckhardt and the Bible," a
marked change from his earlier preoccupation with the
views of H. G. Wells, with whom he had been acquainted
in London (37). The transformation in Sammler's outlook,
apparently influenced deeply by the medieval Christian
theologian, is not a parochial one. Indeed, Eckhardt's belief in God's love of "disinterested purity and unity," antithetical to the Jewish emphasis upon the importance of involvement with life, holds more than a little fascination
for Sammler: "What besides the spirit should a man care
for who has come back from the grave?" (118). However,
the Jewish emphasis upon this world, upon the mundane
aspects of life, is never really far from Sammler's consciousness, for he follows the preceding thought with the observation that "one was always, and so powerfully, so per-
suasively, drawn back to human conditions" (118). Within
the old Sammler there takes place "a second encounter of
the disinterested spirit with fated biological necessities, a
return match with the persistent creature," the opposed
forces represented, though imperfectly, by Meister Eckhardt and the Jewish Bible (118). This juxtaposition of
Christian and Jewish thought, reinforced by the mixed
Catholic-Jewish allegiances of Sammler's daughter, is remindful of the conflicts suffered by Malamud's Frankie Alpine and Yakov Bok, and by Singer's magician, Yasha
Mazur.

Yasha's resolution of the conflict, like that of Malamud's

protagonists, is upon the side of involvement with mankind and the world. Sammler's eulogy for the dead Elya at the novel's end makes clear the extent to which Mr. Sammler too is drawn to this resolution, the transcendent importance he attaches to man's willingness to accept the responsibilities imposed by the code of *mentshlekhkayt*:

> "Remember, God, the soul of Elya Gruner, who as willingly as possible and as well as he was able, and even to an intolerable point, and even in suffocation and even as death was coming was eager, even childishly perhaps . . . even with a certain servility, to do what was required of him. At his best this man was much kinder than at my very best I have ever been or could ever be. He was aware that he must meet, and he did meet—through all the confusion and degraded clowning of this life through which we are speeding—he did meet the terms of his contract. The terms which, in his inmost heart, each man knows. As I know mine. As all know. For that is the truth of it—that we all know, God, that we know, that we know, we know, we know. [313]

The admiration for Elya as *mentsh* that Sammler reveals in the eulogy has, in fact, been expressed earlier, in Sammler's rather lengthy conversation with Angela just before he learns of Elya's death. This conversation makes quite explicit what earlier in the novel is merely suggested, that, despite Sammler's repeated disclaimers, he himself follows the tenets of *mentshlekhkayt*. For, knowing that after Elya's imminent death Angela could very well exercise control over his continued financial support, for Elya's sake Sammler nonetheless risks her fury by suggesting she ask her father's forgiveness for those sexual misadventures which have caused Elya so much pain. Sammler's persistence forces the interchange to a painful climax which leaves him shaking and Angela angry. "He had lost out with Angela, he had infuriated her" (309). She would never forgive him. Sammler had honored his commitment to Elya, very likely at great expense to himself.

In acting as a *mentsh*, Sammler is following his own dictum: "The pain of duty makes the creature upright, and this uprightness is no negligible thing" (220). Related to this attachment to duty is that sense of Sammler's submission to God, perhaps reluctant, which informs and shapes his eulogy and which, indeed, is clearly expressed during his earlier dialogue with Dr. Govinda Lal, author of *The Future of the Moon:* " '. . . being born one respects the powers of creation, one obeys the will of God—with whatever inner reservations truth imposes' " (220). Sammler's acceptance of God with "inner reservations" parallels Herzog's final position, just as the eulogy which closes *Mr. Sammler's Planet* may be regarded as a more explicit and emotional rendering of the meaning conveyed by the silent ending of *Herzog*.

In *Herzog* Bellow deals largely with the Jewish past and the American present; in *Mr. Sammler's Planet* he adds the earthly future. Indeed, space exploration, especially the prospects for human settlement of the moon as an answer to the problems of overcrowding and decay of civilization upon the earth ("New York makes one think about the collapse of civilization, about Sodom and Gomorrah, the end of the world" (304)), emerges as a motif of some prominence in the later novel. The development of this theme leads to the encounter between Sammler and the Indian Lal, professor of biophysics at Imperial College. This meeting, the intellectual watershed of the novel, provides the forum for a friendly testing of sometimes conflicting interpretations of man's history and often dissimilar notions of the possibilities and necessities of his future. Curiously it is the easterner Lal who brings to mind H. G. Wells with the belief that "we cannot manage with one single planet" and his espousal of a Western determination to meet "the challenge of a new type of experience" (219). He places his reliance upon scientific advancement as the best hope for the future of mankind, while Sammler, former confidant of Wells and in some ways a man of Western culture *par excellence*, looks toward man's past. In his desire for limits upon human activity, in his liking for "ceilings," as he puts it, Sammler believes himself to be in essence Jewish and hence Oriental: "Jews, after all, are Orientals. I am content to sit here . . . and watch, and admire the gorgeous Faustian departures for the other worlds" (184). Here once again Sammler reveals a mode of considering the past that is barely distinguishable from that of Herzog, who, as "a Jew, was a born Magian" and "would never grasp the Christian and Faustian world idea, forever alien to [him]" (*Herzog*, 234).

The discussion with Lal culminates in Sammler's own summary of the various stages in his religious evolution: " 'During the war I had no belief, and I had always disliked the ways of the Orthodox. I saw that God was not impressed by death. Hell was his indifference. But inability to explain is no ground for disbelief. Not as long as the sense of God persists. I could wish that it did not persist. The contradictions are so painful' " (236). If a trial of Judaism in the form of a testing of Jewish ideas against Christian thought (as viewed through the prism of Eckhardt's mind) is the result of Sammler's "second encounter" between the physical and the spiritual, we see that the result of a younger Sammler's first encounter (the holocaust) is a trial of God strikingly parallel to that which occurs in Wiesel's chronicling of the Jewish catastrophe. There is the same indictment of God for his failure to uphold the covenant, the same attempt to reject God completely, the same involuntary, unwelcome persistence of belief.

In *Mr. Sammler's Planet* there is, beyond this, the same concern with the idea of madness that is so prominent in the works of Wiesel, particularly in *A Beggar in Jerusalem*. As we have noted earlier, Wiesel describes the struggle of his protagonist against clinical madness, an escape from reality, "an impulse of liberation from the self" (*Town*, 100). Wiesel rejects clinical madness in response to suffering as a betrayal of the responsibilities imposed by the code of *mentshlekhkayt*.

However, there is in Wiesel another notion of madness, that which A. J. Heschel has termed "moral madness," the madness of the ancient Hebrew prophets, the madness that "entails remaining human and retaining a concern for others in a world in which the social norm is hate and indifference." [25] Far from an attempt to flee responsibility in the face of a crushing reality, moral madness characteristically is an expression of refusal to turn away from the struggle to precipitate miracles, to wring meaning from horror. The moral madman is closely linked in spirit to the "absurd man," in the sense of Camus; both are able to face the world's absurdity unflinchingly, with aversion, perhaps, but without denial. Where the absurd man may succeed in doing this on the basis of a rational decision, executed by force of will, the moral madman, like the Hebrew prophets, often acts upon inner compulsion, unable to do otherwise.[26] The beggars in *A Beggar in Jerusalem* are mad in

25. Byron L. Sherwin, "Elie Wiesel on Madness," *Central Conference American Rabbis Journal* (June, 1972), pp. 24–32.

26. A. J. Heschel, *The Prophets*, vol. II (New York, 1962); see especially pp. 223–226.

this sense, possessed by the moral vision of Wiesel's protagonist and philosopher-teachers, who insist upon life as a counter to death, and of those nameless Jewish victims who cling to God in the face of extermination. To varying degrees, Schwarz-Bart's Ernie Levy, Roth's Eli Peck, Malamud's Yakov Bok, and Herzog's friend Nachman, "this gaunt apparition of crazy lecturing Nachman," all display characteristics of the moral madman (*Herzog*, 133).

Mr. Sammler recognizes the two kinds of madness in a mental note: "At the present level of human evolution . . . choices were narrowed down to sainthood and madness. We are mad unless we are saintly, saintly only as we soar above madness" (92–93). This dichotomy between sainthood and madness can be identified with that between moral madness and clinical madness. Referring to "the excuse of madness . . . the blameless state of madness," insisting that "having power destroys the sanity of the powerful," Sammler clearly has in mind the clinical madness of the executioner (89, 218). When he confronts Eisen, who displays "the strength not only of his trade but also of madness" in his attack upon the black man, he is dealing with the clinical madness of a victim-turned-executioner (290). Noting that "madness has always been a favorite choice of the civilized man who prepares himself for noble achievement," Sammler is thinking of moral madness (147).

On the other hand, for Sammler, "registrar of madness," as for the reader, the distinction frequently appears obscured (118). One need only consider these excerpts: "Madness is a base form of the religious life" and "Man is a killer. Man has a moral nature. The anomaly can be resolved by insanity only . . ." (146, 197). The salient but unanswered implicit question is, which insanity is intended here, the insanity which grapples with reality or the one which destroys it? Sammler's tale of "Rumkowski, the mad

Jewish King of Lodz," may in fact be intended as a parable upon the difficulties which attach to distinctions of this kind (230). Rumkowski, appointed *Judenältester* by the Nazis, "was a terror to the Jews of Lodz. He was a dictator . . . —a mad Jewish King presiding over the death of half a million people. Perhaps his secret thought was to save a remnant. Perhaps his mad acting was meant to amuse or divert the Germans" (231). This tale, reminiscent of many tales of the holocaust related by Wiesel, offers no clue to Rumkowski's real motivation, to whether, in Sammler's terminology, he is saint or madman.

In *A Beggar in Jerusalem* madness is inextricably bound up with the Six Day War of June, 1967, and, through it, with the holocaust. Like Wiesel's novel, *Mr. Sammler's Planet* deals with the Six Day War within a framework shaped and moulded by the Jewish catastrophe of the Nazi period, which blunts the Israeli victory, informing it with an aura of horror and sadness. In Wiesel's work the war is illuminated primarily in philosophical-theological terms, with the trial of God, the principal unifying theme of his earlier novels, still very much in evidence. The protagonist of the novel is David, a holocaust survivor, an extension of the survivor-protagonist of the earlier works. After the Israeli capture of the Wailing Wall, Katriel, David's alter ego and philosopher-teacher of the novel, expresses the theological difficulties inherent in the Israeli victory with a reference to the traditional Jewish symbol of mourning: "In order to get here this morning we all had to tear our clothing" (195).[27] Here we find overtones of the same dilemma Wiesel presented in *Dawn:* in order to preserve the Jewish people, it has become necessary to take human life and thus violate the highest Jewish law. The dilemma is expressed by David as well, who speaks of "the shame in-

27. Elie Wiesel, *A Beggar in Jerusalem* (New York, 1969).

herent in survival," admitting that "the victor in me was as alien to me as he was unreal" (*Beggar*, 134, 195). "To die for God and His commandments," Katriel's father explains in his summary of the traditional Jewish view of the matter, "is nothing. . . . But to kill for God . . . is serious and difficult. It is alien to us; it goes against our nature and tradition" (138).

Bellow's reaction to the Six Day War, as expressed by Sammler at any rate, is not so much affected by theological considerations as it is by purely human ones. Despite his advanced age and long-standing indifference to "Jewish affairs," Sammler is powerfully drawn to the scene of the fighting "because for the second time in twenty-five years the same people were threatened by extermination" (*Planet*, 142). Nevertheless, at close range he is overcome by compassion for the Egyptian victims of the fighting, the dead and the captives. Inspecting the battlefields in the guise of a foreign correspondent, Sammler has a close look at the war's human consequences, at the "captured snipers on the bed of a truck, trussed up and blindfolded . . . the desperate faces" (252). There is an implicit reproof of the Israelis in the positive evidence of their use of napalm, a weapon whose use they deny. Unquestionably, "these Jews were tough" (251). In their toughness they not only demonstrate release from the ghetto mentality but raise the possibility that they have abandoned the code of *mentshlekhkayt* as well. Thus the dilemma appears once again: the exterminated forced to kill, the victim forced into the role of executioner.

Sammler's reaction to the Six Day War is unquestionably colored by his own dual role of victim and executioner, just as the fact that he is a survivor profoundly affects his later life. Out of respect for his experiences, his having "returned" from the dead, he is regarded as a prophet, "a

judge and a priest" (91). The invitation to testify against
Eichmann adds to his already impressive stature. On the
other hand Sammler is oppressed by an intangible "heavi-
ness and darkness" of soul that he could not recall "before
1939" (114). He is human, but "in some altered way . . .
at the point where he attempted to obtain his release from
being human" (251), the counterpart of Wiesel's "mes-
sengers from the dead."

Bellow's treatment of the theme of survival in *Mr. Sammler's Planet* parallels that of Wiesel, except for an important difference of tone. A significant clue to this difference is supplied by Sammler, who confesses that he "had
always disliked the ways of the Orthodox" (236), while
Wiesel's protagonist is himself of Orthodox background.
Clearly, the greater reliance upon God leads to the more
poignant and bitter disappointment at his indifference.
There is, moreover, the question of the great dissimilarities
in background of the writers themselves. Bellow's account
of the holocaust can hardly be expected to have the im-
mediacy and emotional power conveyed by the recounting
of Wiesel, himself a survivor. On the other hand, this very
circumstance may account for Bellow's achievement of
artistic distance from the terror and enormity of the holocaust period and the universality of his treatment.

Indeed, it can be argued that while both Wiesel and Bellow to some extent view the holocaust as a paradigm of
the human condition, of man's universal suffering, the emphasis in Wiesel is more specifically directed toward the
tragedy in Jewish terms than is the case with Bellow. If
Wiesel has consistently focused his attention upon the
holocaust itself, as the primary shaping experience of contemporary existence, Bellow has devoted a greater share of
his creative powers to the contemporary experience in general, of which the holocaust forms only a part—thus the

presence of Lal, who is himself a survivor of "the terrible riots" of 1947, "the fighting of Hindus and Moslems . . . called the great Calcutta killing" (210); thus the certainty that "Sammler had not experienced things denied to everyone else. Others had gone through the like. Before and after" (137).

The importance of Eckhardt to the old Mr. Sammler is therefore but one indication that, as compared with the works of Wiesel, even as compared with *Herzog, Mr. Sammler's Planet* may be thought of as an opening out from the specifically Jewish context toward a more universal point of view. And yet, as has been claimed for *Herzog*, it is Artur Sammler "as Jew that gives final credibility to his character." [28] Indeed, Sammler's final act, the eulogy for Elya, confronts the reader with a man who, like his half-Catholic daughter, "couldn't have been more Jewish" (198). Sammler's conviction that "each man knows" the "terms of his contract" indicates his submission to God, his abandonment of the petition "for a release from God's attention" (313, 251). Sammler's "we all know, God, . . . we know" is a prayer "originating far beyond, in the past, of unconscious ancestral origin" (313, 200). In its call for a world governed by the code of *mentshlekhkayt* it is a prayer that is profoundly Jewish, that justifies Judaism as a way of life.

Bellow seems to suggest that if the Jew is alienated in the contemporary world, it is because he has forgotten his origins, grown away from his roots. For the Jew, as for Moses Herzog and Artur Sammler, the Jewish historical consciousness provides a potent counter to doctrines of despair.

28. Flamm, p. 174.

Afterword

Whatever else one may observe about these writers, it is evident that they take Judaism and their Jewishness very seriously, that a "Jewish presence," a sense of continuity with Jewish history, impinges upon their consciousness and finds significant expression in their literary production. This Jewish historical consciousness grows naturally out of the Jewish conception of the nature of man, who "is viewed and understood in Judaism principally by means of the categories of time and history, not of nature." [1] This view of man's nature is inextricably bound up with the evolution of the code of *mentshlekhkayt* and the Jewish communal spirit, the responsibility of man for his fellows: "True history is possible in terms of the group only and not in terms of the isolated individual. The primary unit, the carrier of history, is the community. The individual's destiny is immersed in . . . the destiny of his community." [2] Thus "the collective Jewish ego" of which Alexander Steinbach writes is a genuine, organic force with the power to move men and shape literature. [3]

1. Manfred Vogel, "The Jewish Image of Man and Its Relevance for Today," in Alfred Jospe, ed., *Tradition and Contemporary Experience* (New York, 1970), p. 125.
2. *Ibid.*
3. Alexander Steinbach, "Themes for Jewish Writing," *Jewish Book Annual*, XVI (1958–59), 25.

Indeed, Judaism as a literary force has often received critical attention. Comparing "Eli, the Fanatic" and *The Assistant*, for example, Theodore Solotaroff writes that "in both works there is the similar conversion into the essential Jew," and he makes the observation that "the theme of conversion is a familiar one in Jewish literature." [4] Indeed, conversion in the sense of rededication to Judaism is a prominent feature of many of the works we have discussed here, including *The Last of the Just, The Gates of the Forest,* "Eli, the Fanatic," *Mr. Sammler's Planet,* and, of course, *The Assistant.* The same is true, on a diminished scale, of *The Town beyond the Wall,* which is reminiscent of *The Fixer* in that Michael's ordeal and concomitant moral growth, like Yakov Bok's, take place during his imprisonment under inhuman conditions. It is significant that in every case the conversion or return to Judaism involves primarily moral growth, achievement of *mentshlekhkayt.* Change in religious belief per se, where occurring at all, plays only a secondary role. In every case, too, conversion is closely linked with the trial of Judaism in some form: the trial serves as a vehicle for the conversion, its motive force and setting, and, reciprocally, the conversion, the return to faith, provides a resolution of the trial.

One is able to distinguish three forms of the trial of Judaism: "the trial of God," "the trial of Jewish tradition," and "the trial of the Jews." Since an attack on God contains, by implication, an attack on Jewish tradition, the first two forms are closely related, often appearing together. The first and third are themselves part of ancient Jewish tradition and important features of the Old Testament, where God is berated for man's suffering, and the

4. Theodore Solotaroff, "Philip Roth and the Jewish Moralists," *Chicago Review,* XIII (Winter, 1959), 92, 93.

Hebrews in turn are punished by God for transgressions against his Law. The trial of God occurs most prominently in the novels of Wiesel and Schwarz-Bart, but questioning of God also leads to the moral development of Artur Sammler and of both Yakov Bok and Yasha Mazur. Wiesel and Schwarz-Bart, furthermore, try Jewish tradition insofar as they question the wisdom and relevance of the code of *mentshlekhkayt* itself in the context of the holocaust. A different form of the trial of Jewish tradition is to be found in *Herzog, The Assistant,* and Nelly Sachs's *Eli,* where the tradition is not attacked but tested, in the first two works for its effectiveness as a guide to living and in the third for its power to overcome the overwhelming evil of the holocaust. The trial of the Jews manifests itself in the fiction of Malamud and Roth; here the Jewish community is often condemned for its narrow-minded materialism. A modification of this same theme occurs in Singer's *Satan in Goray,* where the descent into fanaticism is described and attacked. In either case, whether the Jewish community succumbs to materialism or to fanaticism, a loss of *mentshlekhkayt* is involved, and for this the Jewish community is condemned.

It is clear that the trial of Judaism and its concomitant moral questions are widespread literary phenomena, occurring with striking frequency in the fiction produced by contemporary authors of Jewish birth, regardless of often considerable differences of external setting and plot line in their novels. The trial of Judaism, then, emerges as a hallmark of the "Jewish novel" (or "Jewish fiction") as a tangible, easily recognizable pattern in character and plot development which facilitates the classification of particular works as "Jewish," and which helps to establish the "Jewish novel" as a coherent literary genre. This is by no means to assert that the trial of Judaism should be taken as the *exclusive* defining quality of this literary genre, in the sense that only that fiction featuring such a trial is to be identified as "Jewish." Such a definition would exclude the possibility of classifying works of fiction as "Jewish" on the basis of some other set of identifiably Jewish characteristics; this, in my view, would be unduly restrictive and, in the long run, untenable. I do believe, however, that those fictional works which give prominence to a trial of Judaism display a unity of moral outlook and intention which identifies them as representative of a particular, but significant, tendency within the "Jewish novel." The presence of this strain of fiction points to the possibility, at least, that there are other sets of criteria, not touched upon here, for placing specific works within the purview of the "Jewish novel." The existence of such criteria would further delimit and define the "Jewish novel" as genre, and continue the work carried forward here.

Index

"Absurd" universe, 6, 151
Accident, The (Wiesel), 72, 77-81, 85-86, 88
Aleichem, Sholom, 33, 34, 35
American Jewish culture, 19-21; in Roth, 16, 109; in Malamud, 109
American Jewish literature, 1-2, 21-22, 103, 126
Anti-Semitism, 111, 118, 120, 129
Aristotle, 13
Assistant, The (Malamud), 10-11, 14, 103, 109-14
Atheism, 54n

Beggar in Jerusalem, A (Wiesel), 151-52, 153
Bellow, Saul: as Jewish writer, 2, 3, 134-35; God on trial in, 9-10, 137, 150-51; *mentshlekh-kayt* in, 15-16, 128, 129, 131-34, 136, 137, 143, 144, 148-49, 154, 156; theme of moral evolution in, 103; Hasidism in, 126, 133, 134; compared with Wiesel, 126-31 *passim*, 137-41 *passim*, 151-56; on victim-victimizer, 128-29, 139-40, 154; compared with Malamud, 130; *shtetl* in, 130;

holocaust in, 137, 138-39, 153, 155-56; madness in, 152-53; Six Day War in, 154. Works: *Herzog*, 9-10, 127, 129-38, 149, 150; *Mr. Sammler's Planet*, 127, 138-56; *The Victim*, 127-29
Beryll sieht in der Nacht (Sachs), 65

Christianity: compared with *mentshlekhkayt*, 13; in Wiesel, 95-98; in Malamud, 119-22; in Bellow, 147, 150
Conversion, theme of, 158; in Malamud, 10-11, 109-14, 117-25 *passim*; in Singer, 50, 52
Covenant, 9, 11-12, 13, 71; in Wiesel, 9, 13, 71; in Singer, 13, 54-55; in Malamud, 13, 122, 123

Dawn (Wiesel), 72, 76-77, 78, 79-80, 83

Eleazar of Modiim, Rabbi, 12
Eli (Sachs), 4n, 59, 60-65
"Eli, the Fanatic" (Roth), 104-9
"Ethics of the Fathers," 7

Family Moskat, The (Singer), 32

Fixer, The (Malamud), 114-25

Frankl, Viktor, 57

Freud, Sigmund, 24-25, 26

Gates of the Forest, The (Wiesel), 8, 9, 71-74, 79, 89-102

God on trial: and *mentshlekh-kayt*, 7-8, 57, 158-59; in Pentateuch, 8; in Hasidic literature, 8-9; in holocaust literature, 57-60; in Wiesel, 8, 9, 18-19, 58, 59-60, 70-76, 89, 92-94, 99, 100; in Bellow, 9-10, 137, 150-51; in Singer, 31-32; in Sachs, 57, 58-59, 60, 63-64; in Schwarz-Bart, 57, 66, 68; in Malamud, 116-17, 124-25

Greek thought, classical, 13-14

Halper, Albert, 20

Hasidism: and trial of God, 8-9; in Wiesel, 71-73, 79-81, 91-92, 100-102, 126; in Bellow, 126, 133, 134

Haskalah. See Jewish Enlightenment

Heimler, Eugene, 57

Heine, Heinrich, 2

Herzog (Bellow), 9-10, 127, 129-38, 149, 150

Holocaust: literature of, 18-19, 20-22, 56-59; and *mentshlekh-kayt*, 57; in Malamud, 21-22; in Singer, 22; in Wiesel, 56n, 57, 70, 72, 73, 100-101, 155; in Sachs, 57; in Schwarz-Bart, 57, 68-69; in Bellow, 137, 138-39, 153, 155-56

In den Wohnungen des Todes (Sachs), 58

In My Father's Court (Singer), 31

Israel, 77

Jewish-American culture. See American Jewish culture

Jewish-American literature. See American Jewish literature

Jewish Enlightenment, 33

Jewish Wit (Reik), 24-25

"Jewish writing," 1-5, 22-29, 134-35, 157-60

Job, 12-13, 58, 116-17

Just Men, 64, 65-69

Kaddish, 73-74

Kafka, Franz, 2, 3-4, 25-26

Lamed-Vov Zaddikim. See Just Men

Last of the Just, The (Schwarz-Bart), 65-69

Legends of Our Time (Wiesel), 74-75

Lewisohn, Ludwig, 27

Magician of Lublin, The (Singer), 38, 42-55, 103, 115-16

Malamud, Bernard: as Jewish writer, 2, 3; conversion theme in, 10-11, 109-14, 117-25 *passim*; *mentshlekhkayt* in, 11, 14, 15-16, 103-4, 109-10, 111, 113, 114, 117, 119, 120, 123-25; and covenant, 13, 122, 123; influence of holocaust on, 21-22; theme of moral evolution in, 103; on American Jewish culture, 109;

shlemiel in, 110; *shtetl* in, 115; God on trial in, 116-17, 124-25; compared with Bellow, 130. Works: *The Assistant*, 10-12, 14, 103, 109-14; *The Fixer*, 114-25

Mendele Mocher Seforim, 33, 34, 35

Mentshlekhkayt: importance in Jewish writing, 5, 27-28, 29, 103, 157, 158, 159; as ethical code, 6-7, 11-16; and trial of God, 7-10, 159; Job as example of, 12-13; compared with non-Jewish morality, 13-15; in *shtetl* culture, 17-18, 34; in Yiddish classicists, 34; in holocaust, 57; and Just Men, 67; and everyday life, 134

—in Bellow, 15-16; *The Victim*, 128, 129; *Herzog*, 131-34, 136, 137; *Mr. Sammler's Planet*, 143, 144, 148-49, 154, 156

—in Malamud, 15-16, 103-4, 109; *The Assistant*, 11, 14, 109-10, 111, 113; *The Fixer*, 114, 117, 119, 120, 123-25

—in Roth, 103-4; *Portnoy's Complaint*, 14, 16; "Eli, the Fanatic," 104, 105-6, 108-9

—in Nelly Sachs: *Eli*, 61, 62

—in Schwarz-Bart: *The Last of the Just*, 66, 67, 69

—in Singer, 15-16, 35-36, 38, 103; *Satan in Goray*, 38-42; *The Magician of Lublin*, 44, 45, 50, 52, 53, 54

—in Wiesel, 15-16, 151; *The Town beyond the Wall*, 14, 83, 85, 87-88; *The Gates of the Forest*, 74, 75, 89, 91,

94-102 *passim*; *Dawn*, 76-77; *The Accident*, 79

Meshulah, 80

Messiah: traditional Jewish view of, 6; in Singer, 36, 39, 40, 41; in Wiesel, 92-93, 94

Mr. Sammler's Planet (Bellow), 127, 138-56

Night (Wiesel), 58, 72-79 *passim*

Night of the Mist (Heimler), 57

Orthodox Jews, 17

Pentateuch, 8

Peretz, Yitshok, 22-23, 33, 34, 35

Plato, 13

Portnoy's Complaint (Roth), 14, 16

Reik, Theodor, 24-25

Roth, Philip: as Jewish writer, 2, 3; *mentshlekhkayt* in, 14, 16, 103-4, 105-6, 108-9; on American Jewish life, 16, 109; theme of moral evolution in, 103. Works: *Portnoy's Complaint*, 14, 16; "Eli, the Fanatic," 104-9

Sabbatai Zevi, 36, 39, 41

Sachs, Nelly: as Jewish writer, 3; and holocaust, 57, 58, 60; on efficacy of prayer, 59, 60, 64-65; *mentshlekhkayt* in, 61, 62. Works: *Eli*, 4n, 59, 60-65; *In den Wohnungen des Todes*, 58; *Beryll sieht in der Nacht*, 65

Satan in Goray (Singer), 36-37, 38-42

Schwarz-Bart, André: as Jewish writer, 3; and holocaust, 57, 68-69; *mentshlekhkayt* in, 66, 67, 69. Work: *The Last of the Just*, 65-69

Shema, 63

Shlemiel, 110, 146

Shtetl culture, 17-19; in Singer, 30-31, 32-35; in Yiddish classicists, 32-35; in Malamud, 115; in Bellow, 130

Singer, Isaac Bashevis: as Jewish writer, 2, 3; and covenant, 13, 54-55; *mentshlekhkayt* in, 15-16, 35-36, 38-42, 44, 45, 50, 52, 53, 54, 103; influence of holocaust on, 22; *shtetl* in, 30-31, 32-35; and trial of God, 31-32; contrast with Yiddish classicists, 32-35; problem of evil in, 35-38, 41; supernatural in, 35-36; conversion theme in, 50-52. Works: *In My Father's Court*, 31; *The Slave*, 31-32, 37-38, 42; *The Family Moskat*, 32; *Satan in Goray*, 36-37, 38-42; *The Magician of Lublin*, 38, 42-55, 103, 115-16

Six Day War, 153-54

Slave, The (Singer), 31-32, 37-38, 42

Socrates, 14

Souls on Fire (Wiesel), 126

Steinbach, Alexander, 27

Ten Commandments, 32, 54

Town beyond the Wall, The (Wiesel), 14, 72, 81-89, 93

Victim, The (Bellow), 127-29

Wiesel, Elie: as Jewish writer, 2, 3; and trial of God, 8, 9, 18-19, 58, 59-60, 70-76, 89, 92-94, 99, 100; and covenant, 9, 13, 71; *mentshlekhkayt* in, 14, 15-16, 74-79 *passim*, 83, 85, 87-88, 89, 91, 94-102 *passim*, 151; and holocaust, 56n, 57, 70, 72, 73, 100-101, 155; and Hasidism, 71-73, 79-81, 91-92, 100-102, 126; on victims/executioners/observers, 78, 82-84; on suicide, 78-79, 85; suffering as a motif in, 84-86, 100; theme of madness in, 84-85, 86-87, 151-52; philosopher-teachers in, 89-90; problem of evil in, 101; theme of moral evolution in, 103; compared with Bellow, 126-31 *passim*, 137-41 *passim*, 151-56; on Six Day War, 153-54. Works: *The Gates of the Forest*, 8, 9, 71-74, 79, 89-102; *The Town beyond the Wall*, 14, 72, 81-89, 93; *Night*, 58, 72-79 *passim*; *The Accident*, 72, 77-81, 85-86, 88; *Dawn*, 72, 76-77, 78, 79-80, 83; *Legends of Our Time*, 74-75; *Souls on Fire*, 126; *A Beggar in Jerusalem*, 151-52, 153

Yiddish literary tradition, 32-35